MAGNETISE
YOUR EXPERTISE
on **Linked** **in**

I0042875

Discover how to build your business so
you become the only person your prospects
want to work with

NAOMI-ROSE EVERLY

Published by Carrington Noble
7 Bell Yard, London, WC2A 2JR

Email: Naomi@TheProfile.Company
Web: www.TheProfile.Company

IBSN 978-0956-8055-8-4

© Copyright 2024 – Naomi-Rose Everly

Book cover designed by Naomi-Rose Everly

Previously published as The Expert Economy by Naomi Johnson.

The right of Naomi-Rose Everly to be identified as the author of this work has been asserted by her in accordance with the Copyright, Design and Patent Act 1988.

All rights reserved. No part of this publication may be reproduced, stored in a retrieval system or transmitted in any form or by any means, electronic, photocopying, recording or otherwise, without prior permission from the publisher.

This book is sold subject to the condition that it shall not, by way of trade or otherwise, be lend, re-sold, hired out or otherwise circulated without the publisher's consent in any form of binging or cover other than which is published and without a similar condition including the condition being imposed upon the subsequent publisher.

No responsibility for the loss occasioned by any person action or reframing from action as a result of any material in this publication can be accepted by the author or its publisher.

Contents

Introduction

If you sell a service and the promise to solve a problem for your clients, then there is a high chance you're an Expert Entrepreneur. You're likely someone who has spent years mastering your knowledge and capabilities and have a unique take on things.

You see a problem in the world that needs fixing, and you're absolutely adamant it needs fixing your way. So much so you've put everything on the line to strike out on your own and become a solo-entrepreneur.

Your main product is you, your expertise, and your ability to solve your client's problems. You're good at it, and you create transformational results that people talk about. If you could, you'd spend all day working with your clients, researching your subject and talking about it. It's what gets you out of bed in the morning.

Labelling yourself as an 'Expert' can feel a stretch, I know; especially if you've been taught from a young age not to boast and how to fit in. However, the time to stand up for your expertise and know your worth is right now.

As new technology continues to transform our world and how we do business, a new economy is emerging, and a new type of entrepreneur for whom the challenges and risks of building a business are very different. With this, comes the need for a radically different approach to marketing.

In this book, you'll be introduced to a step-by-step methodology designed to quickly position you as the 'go-to' expert within your industry and get paid for the value you create.

Promoting ourselves as an 'expert' might feel a little uncomfortable at first, but the more we show up and solve our client's problems, the more our confidence will grow. Every time we see our client succeed, and every time we see relief on a person's face because we have provided the solution they have been looking for, we are rewarded.

Whether you remain in full-time employment moving within roles internally, or whether you undertake short contracts or projects on a freelance basis, or within your own business, the need to be able to communicate our value and monetise your skills is imperative.

The Gig Economy vs The Expert Economy

You've probably heard of the Gig Economy, the term used for the increasing number of people taking up short term contracts and freelance assignments. The first thing I want to say here is that this is not you.

People who undertake gigs perform functional tasks. They come in, deliver the result and leave. They are hired to perform a function that is part of a bigger picture, but they do not hold the vision or the direction for the end result. They aren't responsible for the final output. They are only responsible for delivering what is asked of them on any given day.

They are actors on the stage that come in to play a role and could easily be replaced by someone who looks just like them. They might build the stage, but they didn't create the vision for it, and they aren't responsible for the final product. They are more than skilled at what they do. They are very talented and able to deliver excellent work, and it's that which gets them hired back.

But it isn't why you are hired.

As an Expert Entrepreneur, you see the bigger picture, and you're responsible for it. You know how to direct the play, how to hire in the actors, how to bring the vision to life, and how to make it perform.

You're there from the beginning of the project, right through to the end. No matter what. Your project may be a small cog in a big machine, but you're responsible. You've been given the reigns, and your word is final. You are the expert, and no one questions the wisdom you bring. People look to you for advice; confident that you know what you're talking about - and it's why you were hired.

That's not to say you have all the answers. It's to say that you have the knowledge and experience to flex and innovate to deliver the win, no matter what obstacles are thrown up at you.

An expert is 50% knowledge and experience, and 50% intuition.

There are two types of Expert

In my view, there are two types of expert:

Thought-Leader

An expert in their industry who shares their perspective on industry developments and is prepared to challenge the status quo.

A Trusted Advisor

An expert who is prepared to spend time with their client to understand their unique challenges and then provide the very best advice and support implementing that advice.

Each of us is a combination of both. How much of each will depend on our industry, what we are promoting, our role within the business and where we feel most comfortable.

There is, of course, another type of person here, and that is the influencer. You'll most certainly know of many - perhaps in your industry. You might want to be like them, or the thought of having a 'following' might make your stomach turn - I know it makes mine turn.

An **Influencer** is someone who enjoys a special status within their industry because when they speak, people listen. When their name is associated with a project, the project is bound to succeed. Doors open, opportunities flood in and people scramble to be involved. They get to write their own terms, receive VIP status wherever they go and get to be part of the best teams.

Sounds good right?

It certainly does… but it depends on how you achieve it!

People establish influence in a variety of ways. They may be a celebrity who has built their status through their work, such as an actor or a well-known business entrepreneur like Richard Branson.

Or they may be a celebrity-influencer, someone who has built influence by establishing a social media following simply by being themselves. They add value because they entertain their audience with new content. They are paid well to promote a product or service because, when they say something is good, people buy it, but they have no actual skill or service of their own to market. If their popularity falls or their reputation is tarnished, their income goes too.

The other type of influencer is someone who has flooded social media with a prolific amount of content, from which they have become well known. Their content may be forward-thinking, disruptive and catchy. They may have had a level of success in the past that people want to tune in and learn about, or they may have a product or service that solves a problem everyone has, so people are talking about them.

What's interesting about this type of influencer is that they are respected simply because they are known. The more people talk about them, the more they are seen, and the more they are seen, the more they are respected and revered. They sell their products and make money. The more money they make, the more they are put up on a pedestal and, dare I say it, worshipped.

The problem with this type of status, however, is what it takes to achieve this level of influence and whether what is behind it has any substance.

This is why I say, 'one strategy does not fit all'.

For the Expert Entrepreneur, this level of exposure can feel intimidating and achieving it distracting. You are someone who has spent years submerged in your industry and is passionate about delivering transformational results for your clients. Just the idea of having to promote videos on social media and organise marketing campaigns is exhausting.

It's not what you are built for.

Yet, it is the marketing strategy you are taught to follow by the people with the gravitas to grab your attention and teach you.

A few years ago, I got to co-host an event with a well-known celebrity entrepreneur. We both had 45-minutes to speak to the audience and share our subject expertise. My co-host was invited to share his journey to success and what it involved. What struck me was his definition of success, and how he was teaching others marketing strategies to help them achieve the same results - on the assumption that they actually wanted these results.

His basic premise was that his business is absolutely brilliant because he had a good flow of new clients and a team in place to service them. The product is clear, the systems are set up, the marketing works, and he gets to sit back and do what he enjoys all day long. Doesn't that sound great?

It does until you find out what he enjoys doing all day long.

In reality, he isn't just sitting back, watching new clients flowing in. His enjoyment isn't playing golf all day long. His enjoyment is marketing, and his business is a marketing agency. He enjoys sitting back and marketing the business, while everyone else fulfils the new contracts coming in.

...which basically means the new contracts are coming in because he is marketing all day. This is absolutely excellent. I applaud him. I really do.

...the problem is, though, he enjoys marketing.

...and not only that, he is a trained marketing professional who runs a marketing agency

If you're a marketing expert, of course, you're going to enjoy this.

For most Expert Entrepreneurs, though, being able to do marketing every day is not the holy grail. It is not the end point. It is not the destination that says we have "made it". In fact, it is the opposite.

If we follow this path to success, we'll end up the same. Marketing all day long. And will we enjoy it? Is that our definition of 'sitting back and doing what we love all day long'? Not unless you're a marketing professional.

If you're anything like me and the experts I work with, an ideal day is having the opportunity to deliver transformational results for our clients and solving meaningful problems in the world. We want to be at the coal face doing the work.

We want to be at the forefront of the industry, working on the most challenging problems, evolving our skills along with the industry, and contributing to exciting conversations with other industry leaders. We submerged in our topic, and we love it.

"One of the biggest problems I have witnessed, time and time again, is Expert Entrepreneurs become worn out by the need to market their business. They become so distracted by the steep learning curve they are no longer the leading expert in their industry or fulfilled in their work."

The last thing we want to do is spend our time doing marketing. Any marketing. At all. In fact, if we could do away with it altogether, we would.

Our businesses are time-sensitive and fast-paced. The truth is, we can only call ourselves a business because we had to set up a company for tax purposes, and we only call ourselves 'entrepreneurs' because we have a business - and even that feels like a stretch.

Would we just prefer to get on with the job of delivering transformational results for our clients and studying our subject? With our invoices magically paid at the end of the month?

This notion of having to market our businesses, share content on social media and make videos that all fit nicely into a sales campaign is the worst part of setting up on our own.

So why then do I call you an 'Entrepreneur', when I know for a fact that you most probably don't identify as one?

The reason is that, as you embark on the journey of figuring out how to win new clients, you're going to come across a lot of teachers with fancy marketing strategies to invest in that will seem great at the beginning but quickly get you off track.

You will come to know of yourself as an Entrepreneur, and you will tune into content that supports and helps entrepreneurs.

The trouble is, though, one strategy does not fit all, and it's imperative that you know what type of entrepreneur you are if you're going to succeed. It's also imperative that you know how to invest your time and money wisely, taking on training courses and marketing projects that are right for your type of entrepreneurship and doing so at the right time.

That's what I want to be here to help you to figure out.

I want to help you to discover not only the type of **expert** you are, but also the type of **entrepreneur** you are, so you select the right marketing strategies for you.

Strategies that will help you remain true to your calling and fulfilled in work - rather than someone who has become so entrenched in marketing strategy that they are no longer an expert in their industry. Because, believe me, it happens. And the fall out isn't pretty.

Instead, I want to help you balance building influencer status with making real money, with the pick of industry-leading projects to choose from.

I want to help you decide where your influencer strategy starts and where it stops. What fits right for you, and what's right for your clients.

I want to teach you the nuisances that may seem small but are the difference between thriving in your business and game-over. The differences that will see prospects seeking you out, hanging on your every word, and coming to you pre-sold and ready to buy at any price you name.

It's not hard work—It's smart work. It requires designing your business in just the right way, so it generates leads and works for you, behind the scenes, while you're delivering the transformational results people talk about.

Sounds interesting?

Well, my utopia is a world where experts get to spend 70% of their time working with clients, 20% of their time studying to remain an expert in their industry, and 10% of their time managing their business.

Where do sales and marketing come in? Well, that's the magic I want to teach you!

It happens when your sales and marketing become a natural overflow of your study time - and trust me, it'll feel as natural and as exciting to you as you find sitting down after a long week to learn more about your subject.

Audience. Lifestyle. Personality.

If you've been in this industry for any amount of time, then you'll know just how many marketing strategies there are and training courses to match. It can be tempting to do them all, especially if you've sat in a big marketing conference for experts or attended a webinar listening to the seller promote the magic of the strategy and the wonderful results you will achieve. If you've read my book "Grassroots to Green Shoots," you'll know that I too fell foul of that and just how much it cost me.

The truth is, any marketing strategy, whether Instagram, YouTube, podcasting, Facebook Ads, or LinkedIn, requires a level of mastery. To get results, you have to be consistent. You have to learn the basics and keep showing up until you have mastery. You have to keep going, no matter the challenges and the failures, until you figure out how to make it work for you. And this requires investment. Not just in your time but also in a specialist to help you navigate the roadblocks and difficulties when they come up. Thus, it requires a commitment, a commitment that will not be shaken no matter what happens.

Unfortunately, few of us have this. Not because we're not good at commitments but because we don't have the confidence – or the guidance – to stick with a strategy no matter what until it works. When things don't seem to be working out, we usually get distracted – without realising it. We'll attend another webinar or conference and find the next shiny thing promising all the results. We'll forget that we invested £3,000 for a mentor to help us write a book, or £1,500 to attend an eight-week course on creating YouTube videos. And before we know it, we have a little bit of knowledge about a lot of things but no actual results.

How do we solve this? By first getting absolutely sure of our marketing strategy before we invest in it so we stick with it no matter what new marketing methods present themselves.

How do we identify it? By identifying what is right for our audience, lifestyle, and personality.

Audience

Where do our ideal clients show up? And what do they engage with? There is no point running Facebook Ads if your target audience Is CEOs of major corporates. Not only are they unlikely to spend time on Facebook to see them, but they are also very unlikely to be impressed with your three-step sales process and attend an online webinar. This type of person typically does not put their details into a form to get a free download or attend a webinar, nor manage their own email inbox to read follow-up emails. Or perhaps they will for your content? This is something you'll need to be explore.

Before creating any marketing strategy, it is important to consider the personality and lifestyle of your target market and understand what they engage with and how. Your brand, your approach, and your message have to align perfectly, or else it will fail.

Lifestyle

How much time do you have? Some marketing strategies are time-consuming and can require more time than you have available. For example, a good LinkedIn Carousel can take 3 hours to create, and if you don't have creative skills, still look terrible and fail to hit the mark. A 4-minute YouTube video could take 10 hours to complete, and if you need to make one each week, you may find you don't have the time to keep it up to gain the following that you need.

If you are someone who has left full-time work to have more flexibility, or you're intending to work part-time, you may find you've committed to a marketing strategy that has you working more hours than you were before or intend to.

Personality

Does it come naturally to you? Do you enjoy it? If you're an introvert or someone who likes to hide in the background, maintaining an Instagram following may become difficult. When we feel the hype of a strategy, we can throw everything into it, but when the hype wears off or we feel knocked by life, are we going to maintain the strategy with the consistency needed to reap the rewards of our investment? If the answer is no, our efforts will be short-lived, and we'll likely move on to the next shiny thing to avoid having to do what no longer feels comfortable.

With all these things, we may conclude that it just didn't feel right or that it wasn't working. When in truth, we gave up. Not because we're quitters but because it wasn't the right strategy four our audience, lifestyle or personality. As experts who aren't natural marketers, and there will be a lot of things that don't feel right – or aren't right- and that is why finding the right strategy is so important.

The right marketing strategy could be as simple as attending a networking event every quarter, following up for coffee with people, and hosting monthly lunches with four-or-so people who can become referral partners. You may have already built up enough flow for your business that this is all that is needed to maintain it.

The right marketing strategy could be a YouTube channel or producing your own podcast, either alone or by collaborating with others who deliver the same services as you. Before deciding, it is imperative that you fully explore these questions, ideally with a professional who can reflect back to you and give you insights about what you are considering that you may not have considered.

However, whichever method you choose, there is one platform that for us as experts, is vital to master, and that is LinkedIn.

Why LinkedIn?

When it comes to building a business as a lone entrepreneur, I think there is little doubt that LinkedIn is a valuable tool for building our influence and attracting new prospects to our business.

The question is, though, how do you do it?

With so many training courses on the market these days, there is probably little variety in the advice provided. It's the normal rhetoric. However, one strategy most certainly doesn't fit all.

And when it comes to the expert entrepreneur whose time is limited and whose expertise lies in their industry profession, not in their ability to market their services, getting to grips with LinkedIn and making it work involves a lot more than posting interesting content and accepting invitations.

Instead, it requires designing a business that can generate leads and work for you in the background while you deliver the core of your services to paying clients.

With generating new business as a solo-entrepreneur firmly at the heart of this book, I am going to show you how to design your business, so your most ideal clients come to you pre-sold and ready to buy – and all within a day's work.

To do it, we're going to focus on using LinkedIn because, with more 650 million users globally and recognised as a business platform, LinkedIn affords us the opportunity to market our expertise for a relatively low cost.

And before you ask, everything I teach within this book can be achieved with a free LinkedIn account, meaning you don't need to invest any more money in marketing to achieve the results outlined in this book. You just need to apply it.

Also, the strategies will easily transfer to other social media platforms.

A Point of Warning

While a LinkedIn strategy is important, doing all of it might not be. With any strategy, the goal is to win new clients, and we win new clients when we have warm leads. Thus, if you already have ideal clients reaching out to you via other means, perhaps by being a keynote speaker or by being a guest on a podcast, and you haven't the capacity to get back to them, allocating time to creating content for LinkedIn will not be a priority.

Why? Because LinkedIn warms cold prospects up and, in truth, may never fully warm them up to the point where they want to work with you. As you'll see as we read on, not everyone is an ideal client. They may not have the budget, time, authority, or need to purchase your services. So, using up your available capacity to produce content for them when you have super hot leads waiting for you to get back to them is not going to be a good use of time.

Unfortunately, though, you may continue to feel the pressure to do so, adding it to your to-do list every day and watching the goal slip away each quarter when you review your progress. My view? Take it off the list.

Producing content is great when you have the capacity or a team to help you, and trust me, the influencers out there with the most engagement have a team of people helping them produce high-quality content every day. And if they don't, well, we can't see behind the screen to see how many hours they are working or how they are balancing client work with content creation. So, we shouldn't compare ourselves to them or create a false pressure.

What we need to know is what is right for us. As we'll see later, LinkedIn algorithms change all the time, and producing the level of content required to build a following and achieve high engagement on our posts daily is a strategy within itself and may not be right for us, as discussed above. The purpose of this book is to put all this into perspective so you can do what's right for your business without looking over your shoulder, feeling pressure to do something, or worrying that you've missed something.

Who am I?

So, who am I, and why should you listen to me? Well, firstly, I've been in the entrepreneurial game of selling my time for money for over a decade now. I got started in 2006 before LinkedIn had reached UK shores, and Facebook and YouTube were yet to get started.

My first business was as a life-coach, and throughout two and a half years, I made every mistake in the book. I won't bore you with what I did here as you can easily read about it in my book Grassroots to Green Shoots available on Amazon.

It was in 2012 that my journey with LinkedIn began. A business colleague of mine called me to ask if I'd join his sales team. Quickly recognising the opportunity for what it was, I jumped at the chance to be part of this fledgeling new start-up selling LinkedIn training. The founder, Bert Verdonck, was already well known within the space, having been accredited as the first certified LinkedIn trainer and co-author of the best-selling book 'How to Really Use LinkedIn'.

For two years, I worked with the team providing 30-minute LinkedIn profile reviews demonstrating the value of LinkedIn with a view to selling training courses. During this time, I spoke with hundreds of individuals, learning about their businesses, and giving advice on how to position themselves on LinkedIn. Only I found I was continually repeating myself.

So, knowing how to fix this, I wrote my book 'What to Put on Your LinkedIn Profile', also available on Amazon.

However, when the company began a formal partnership with LinkedIn, hosting the 'Rock Your Profile' stand at their EMEA conference in 2013 & 2014, I started to realise it was time to part ways.

My passion for helping solo-entrepreneurs to position themselves as the 'go-to' expert in their industry and build their business was growing; something that was close to my heart, having failed on my original journey.

My favourite phone calls were always with the passionate entrepreneurs who, like me, had put everything on the line to follow the road less travelled and cultivate a life worth living.

I found myself continually pulling in my training from Daniel Priestley's course Key Person of Influence during my profile reviews, and I wanted to do more of it.

Then in an unexpected turn of events in 2015, I found myself with the decision to either get a new job or start my own business. The latter being something I had promised I would never do again. Yet, I could see I had a solution that people needed.

For all the years providing LinkedIn Profile Reviews, I was yet to find someone who would actually apply what I told them and do it well. So, I began asking people if they would prefer if I just did it for them. The answer was yes.

So very much against the idea of having my own business again but needing to make fast cash, I got started. Only I had no money in the bank, no ability to borrow, and the rent was due in two weeks.

Knowing that our environment dictates performance, I opted to take what money I did have to hire a desk at the local innovation centre. However, one-night walking home from the office, I began questioning my choices, asking, 'But what if this doesn't work? What will I do?' Having just moved to Portsmouth seven months before, I didn't know many people. My previous role was London focused and hadn't afforded me many opportunities to network locally.

Suddenly I realised that "What will I do if this doesn't work out?" was the wrong question. I stopped in my tracks and said it again "wrong question". All my years of personal development kicked in, and I realised I needed to ask myself better questions.

So, instead, I asked, "How do I make this work?"

I ran some quick calculations. If I wanted to earn £4k per month, I would have to sell ten profiles at £400 per person. To sell ten profiles, I would need to make approximately 40 presentations to ideal prospects (fast!). If I wanted to make 40 presentations, I needed to share my message with approximately 120 people.

I didn't have a list, and I didn't have time.

So, I asked myself, 'How can I get in front of 120 people fast?"

Speaking Engagements.

"Who do I know that would give me a speaking slot with my ideal audience?"

Immediately, the leader of a local networking group came to mind.

I gave him a call and asked if I could speak at his breakfast meeting. As luck would have it, he'd had a cancellation, and he invited me to give a talk the next week.

Just as I was beginning, another local business network leader approached me, asking if I would speak at their open meeting the next week. Of course, I said yes.

Within two weeks, I had spoken to 120 people.

During my talks, I added value. I provided lots of insights and practical tips. I shared how LinkedIn is a vital part of your marketing mix, and the importance of making sure it pitches you, your business, and your expertise perfectly.

I offered attendees a free LinkedIn Profile Review.

I had over forty business cards. Following up with each one, I held back-to-back meetings, focused on getting to know each business owner, and providing tailored feedback and insight so the prospect could write their own LinkedIn profile.

I told each person exactly what *they should do* and then asked whether that was something they felt they could do for themselves or whether they needed me to help them.

Ten people said yes. Then another ten.

By my fourth month, I was at capacity. I had far exceeded my goal of selling 10 LinkedIn Profiles per month.

In my fifth month, my name came up in all the right conversations at a marketing agency in High Wycombe. Before I knew it, I was invited to write 40+ LinkedIn profiles for Oracle in the USA and Europe.

Connecting with each person I met and being consistent with my actions on LinkedIn, the leads came rolling in. Sometimes fast and sometimes slow, depending on what I need at any given time.

But this wasn't by luck or by chance.

This was a formula.

A formula that starts with how you structure your business and combines online and offline strategies to get you in front of ideal prospects, in just the right way, that they not only buy from you but talk about you.

A formula I now teach to my clients and is detailed in this book.

Let me introduce you to Stacey.

Back in October, four months after the UK decision to leave the European Union, Stacey reached out to me via LinkedIn because her business was in a period of severe decline, and she had no idea what to do about it. Before then, she had had plenty of clients scattered across Europe, but with Brexit, many of the clients decided that working with a UK agency was a bad look for them.

Overnight, Stacey had lost her business, and it appeared, her ability to get new ones.

Her old methods for finding new business were no longer working. She couldn't rely on word-of-mouth, and speculative phone calls to ideal prospects weren't producing the results the way they once had. Stacey realised quickly that the game had changed and so must she.

Curious about LinkedIn, Stacey called me.

Together, we applied the principles and strategies in this book, within three months, added £200k to Stacey's pipeline and secured £45k worth of new business.

We did this by focusing Stacey's message around the problem she solves for her clients and positioning her as the 'go-to' expert within her industry for this problem.

With a clear LinkedIn profile, a concise download, and a few tweaks to her website, Stacey began sharing interesting content on LinkedIn and connecting with ideal prospects. Together, we carefully crafted her inbox messages, so they were genuine and authentic and built a rapport.

Just four months after starting our work together, Stacey received a message from an internationally renowned institution asking if she was available to complete a project for them. They said they were impressed with the quality of her download and her offer and were ready to go ahead immediately if she was willing.

Stacey nearly fell over herself. Just four months before, she had been cold calling this organisation trying to win their business, and now they were approaching her.

Just as predicted, her ideal prospects are now coming to her pre-sold and ready to buy. Stacey is thrilled with the results we've achieved together.

Results you too can achieve with this simple formula.

The formula I outline in this book.

If you're a solo entrepreneur selling your time for money and want a simple formula for winning new business quickly, then I invite you to come on this journey with me.

In this book, I outline the strategy from beginning to end, but if at any point you feel that you need personalised help implementing the strategy or would like to take the learning deeper, I invite you to reach out.

Along with this book is an online training course with the potential for one-to-one coaching if you need it. Should you need added inspiration during the week or first thing Monday morning, you can also dip in and out with my Podcast, also called The Expert Economy which can be found on all major hosting sites.

So let's get started.

Are you an Expert Entrepreneur?

Do you have specialist skills or expertise in a particular field?

Do you enjoy learning more about your topic?

Do you enjoy solving people's problems within your area of expertise?

Learn more and gain further insights by visiting
www.TheExpertEconomy.com/Quiz

TAKE THE SCORECARD

Discover how well your business measures up against the strategies and insights discussed in this book by taking our scorecard.

Upon completion, you will receive a complimentary one-page business planner that encapsulates everything covered in the book and evaluates your performance across these critical areas.

The planner is designed to provide a concise overview, aiding you in identifying strengths and areas for improvement, ensuring your LinkedIn strategy is as effective as possible.

Go to **http://www.theprofile.company/scorecard**

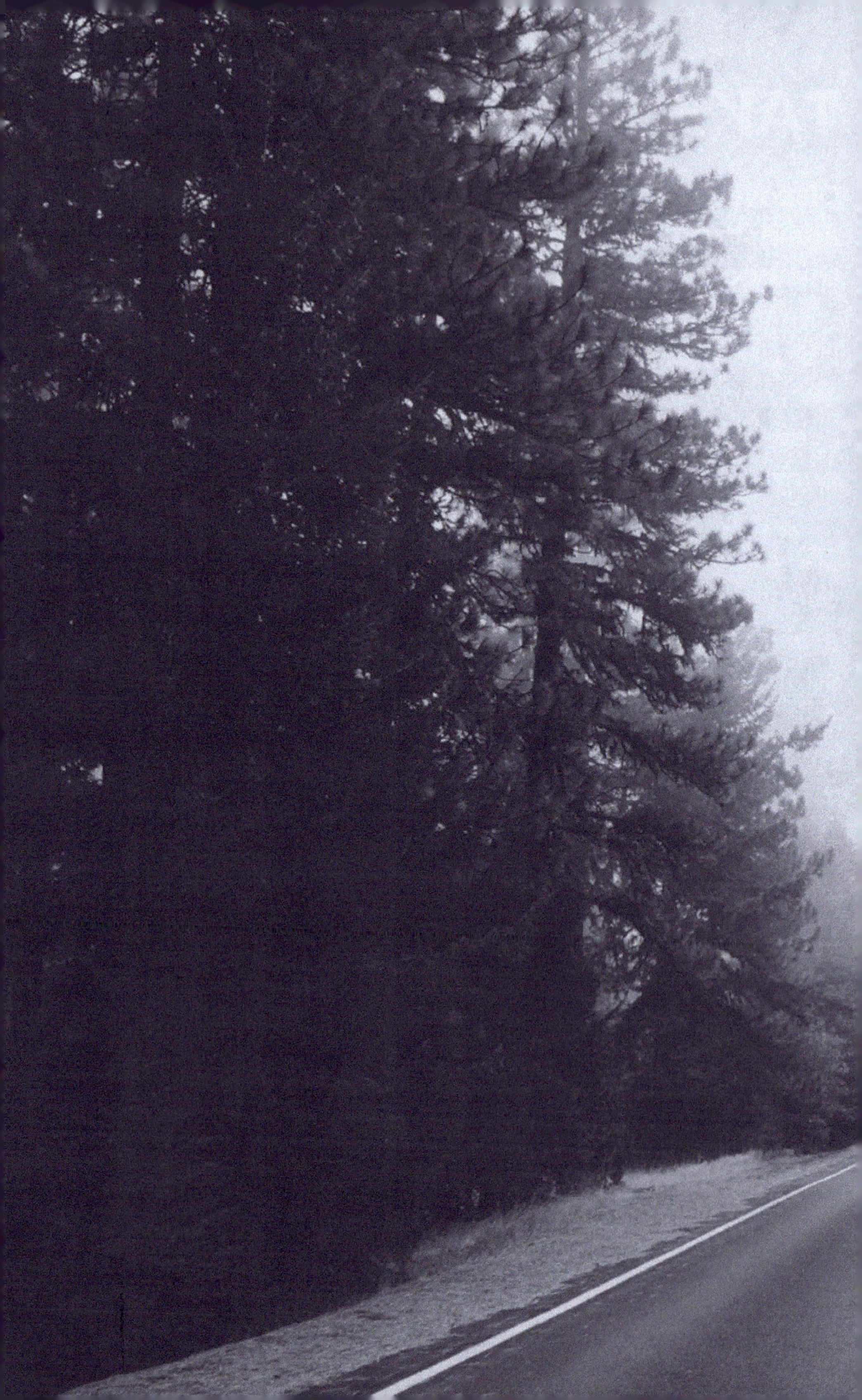

Begin with the End In Mind

1. Begin with The End in Mind

In his legendary book 'The Seven Habits of Highly Successful People," Stephen Covey summed it up perfectly. You have to begin with the end in mind. And when it comes to building your business with LinkedIn, there has never been a truer statement.

The general industry advice is that if you want to achieve results on LinkedIn, you need to invest 9-minutes a day (45-minutes a week). LinkedIn is, however, an arcade of choices and distractions that if you're not careful, will eat up your entire day. If you don't have direction and a clear outcome, your 9-minutes a day is likely to disappear quickly, leaving you with nothing to show for your time.

To use those 9-minutes well, you need to know your outcome. You need to ask yourself 'what am I here to achieve?'

Your outcome is sales

It might sound crass, or even counterintuitive, but if we're logging into LinkedIn during the working day and we're not looking for a full-time job, then our objective for being on LinkedIn is to win new sales. Even though we might tell ourselves that we are there to connect, interact and keep up to date on industry news and activities, we are doing these activities as a prelude to winning new business. We're just doing them without any direction or focus.

The difference is we just haven't connected the dots and become intentional about it. With a little forethought and planning, we can make those activities deliver a result.

Selling via social media is not the done thing

In 2009, with the rise of social media, the word 'Defriend' or 'Unfriend' became one of the most popular new words in the English language and was probably uttered by just about anyone with a social media account.

It's the term we use to describe the need to disconnect or unfollow a person on a social media account and is usually reserved for those who violate social protocol by clogging up our walls with useless content; or worse, outright selling.

However, if we want to build our businesses using LinkedIn, we want to lead our target audience to not just engage with us but buy from us. If we are on LinkedIn to build our businesses, we are on there to sell.

We are there to win new clients, yet we must do it without selling.

So how exactly do we do this if we're not supposed to sell outright? I think we can all agree, receiving a message from someone we don't know or have just connected with, who immediately pitches their services, is pretty annoying. So, what is the right thing to do?

The logic is very simple.

In time-sensitive businesses, we have to consider how we are investing our time and question our every move. We don't have big marketing budgets, we don't have time to waste on activities that don't produce results. We must produce results. Results that generate cash.

We do this by establishing our self as an Expert within our industry, so when a prospect is ready to buy, they know to come to us. We do this by talking about the problem we solve, and the symptoms of the problem and the consequences of not solving it.

We do it by being very clear what we stand for, by pitching our services clearly and leading prospects through a staged process that leads them naturally through to the point where they can opt in to buy from us.

When we do this well, our marketing becomes effortless, and prospects come to us pre-sold.

Sales Require Sales Appointments

Unless you sell fast-moving consumer goods, it is unlikely that you'll make sales without speaking to your prospect. Today, it is perfectly normal to google a product, read the reviews and then make our buying decision independently. We no longer require a sales representative to get involved, and, in most cases, simply don't have the time or patience for them.

However, when buying a service, we do need to speak to someone. And when selling a service, we need to spend time with our prospect to find out who they are and if we can help, and perhaps more importantly, that we want to. Thus, we need to speak to our prospect before a sale can be made, and we can do this by either talking to them on the phone or meeting with them face-to-face.

> **"…when selling a service, we need to speak with our prospect to find out who they are and if we can help, and perhaps more importantly, that we want to."**

A few months ago, a prospect asked me to generate leads for her on LinkedIn. I walked her through the general principles and how we might approach this together, and then she asked "How do I know you'll get me results? I've been burned before by people saying they'd generate me new business but haven't."

My answer was honest and straightforward. I can't. It was clear that she wasn't expecting this answer, so I explained.

I told her; marketing alone won't win you business. It's what you do with an interested prospect that counts. Winning new business takes a lot more than simply being active on social media and attending networking meetings.

First, you need to have a product or service that solves a real problem, one that people are willing to pay money for. It requires you to pitch your service just right, so your prospect sits up and takes notice.

Second, it requires you to establish trust and familiarity with your prospect, so they feel confident hiring you. Third, it requires you to respect the psychology of how people buy and walk each new prospect through the buying decision process, so they feel able to make the right purchase for them - and not just the one that is right for you.

Therefore, when we're active on LinkedIn, we need to focus our attention on building our reputation as an industry expert, so our name comes up in all the right conversations. We need to build relationships with our ideal prospect and add value, so they get a feel for the quality of our service and the results we achieve for our clients. It is only when we have achieved this that a prospect will wave their hand and opt-in to our first offer, a sales appointment. Typically, a prospect won't opt-in for a sales appointment because they don't want to be sold to. Therefore, we have to pitch the conversation in such a way that it becomes attractive and something they want to give their time up for.

It is because of all these things that I told my prospect, that while my approach would generate leads for her, I couldn't guarantee she'd win new business; as winning new business depends upon her ability to successfully hold a sales conversation. Something, as an Expert Entrepreneur, no one can do for her.

Time Sensitive Businesses

We've already mentioned the importance of focusing our efforts when our business is time-sensitive, and when it comes to sales, this is vitally important.

In our businesses, the last thing we want is to waste time speaking to a prospect who is calling to ask basic questions they could quickly have learned online. We want to avoid lengthy conversations that have no conclusion and pushing our product on people who aren't interested.

We simply don't have time, as time is money. In our business, we want to find that 'sweet spot' where prospects come to us 'pre-sold'. They know they have a problem, they like our solutions, and they trust us to deliver. They have the budget to invest, and they are on the verge of doing so.

Research carried about by LinkedIn and Altimeter in 2012 discovered that the modern-day buyer now makes 57% of their buying decision online before reaching out to a sales representative. We just need to look at the change in our own behaviour to recognise this statistic is pretty accurate.

As a business owner and/or salesperson, our job is to reverse engineer our prospects' decision-making process and build a sales process that supports them at each stage of their buying journey. We need to meet them at just the right moment, with just the right content, just as they are identifying they have a problem and evaluating how to fix it.

When we do this, we are in the perfect position to become their Trusted-Advisor.

A Trusted Advisor is someone we recognise as knowledgeable and experienced in a given field, and that we trust to answer our questions accurately and honestly, with no hidden agenda.

By sharing valuable content that helps the prospect understand precisely what they need and how to buy, we position ourselves as a Trusted Advisor. Someone they can trust to provide great information that they can rely on.

"As a Trusted Advisor, people trust us to provide information they can rely on with no hidden agenda."

If our information resonates with them, they will want to know more and how they can work with us. It is at this point that our prospect will be most open to having a conversation with us and finding out we can help them, i.e. Sales Appointment.

If they don't like our product or just feel it isn't right for them, we can part company knowing that we have helped them gain more clarity about what they want and need, even if that means helping them to understand their problem better and referring them to another service provider or our 'competitor'.

With 57% of a buying decision being made online, the final 43% represents the sales appointment. If we have completed the above stages successfully, the prospect will come to the conversation open to hearing what we have to say and open to learning about our solution.

Thus, we need to develop our online content to match where our prospect is in their buying decision. It needs to take them from not knowing they have a problem and needing a solution (0%) to knowing they have a problem and being ready to invest in a solution (57%).

Book Sales Appointments

When you build your LinkedIn strategy around meeting your prospects where they are at in their buying decision and then helping them to make the right decision for them, everything will fall into place.

Your 9-minutes a day on the platform suddenly has a purpose. A purpose that drives how you invest your time on the platform in a way that will generate the results you want from it.

As I've said, the outcome is to win new business. However, it is how we approach our prospect that determines whether they will view us as a nuisance to 'unfriend' or see us as a valuable addition to their network that they want to hear from.

This is the difference that makes all the difference.

It's the difference between having sales appointments that feel uncomfortable and are a hard slog, to ones that flow naturally and convert into paid business.

Make Sales Predictable

When you get this just right, sales become predictable. You'll know precisely what you need to do to produce the level of sales you need. It's a concept my mentor Daniel Priestley calls LAPS:

Leads. Appointments. Presentations. Sales.

Leads are the number of prospects engaging with your content. *Appointments* are your sales conversations; a structured conversation, whether face-to-face, via the phone or online, that provides the opportunity to *Present* your offer to the prospect and invite the *Sale.*

Not everyone you have an appointment with wants to hear your presentation, and that is OK. As you explore the person's issues, you might find you aren't the right person to help them, or that their problem isn't big enough to justify an investment in a service such as yours. You can offer some tips and pointers and happily send the person on their way, knowing that you've added value.
Having sales conversations become a lot easier when you lead with your expertise and help people. If someone has a big enough issue that requires investing in, you'll know because you won't be able to fix their problem within half an hour.

Now aware of the extent of their problem and impressed with what you've been able to highlight to them, there is a very high chance the prospect will ask you how you can help and to pitch your services. Being invited to pitch your services is far nicer than feeling that you're 'selling' to a person who doesn't want you to.

If they don't ask or you both feel that there isn't a good match, there is a very high chance that the person will go on to tell others about you. Now aware of the issues surrounding their challenges, they'll likely meet others in the same situation. Equipped with the insights you've given them, they'll be able to talk on your subject with some authority and help someone else understand the challenges they are facing, creating an ideal prospect for you.

Knowing when to say no

Turning people away, and being selective who you work with, gets more comfortable to do when you have priced your packages appropriately, and you know how many clients you can take on.

As an Expert Entrepreneur in a time-sensitive business, our goal is to create a transformational product and price it so we only need to sell two packages per month to achieve our financial target, something we'll cover in more detail later.

This means we will only want two new sales per month. To win two new sales, with the right sales process in place, you'll need approximately ten sales appointments.

With numbers like that, it makes hearing 'no' eight times much easier to handle.

Therefore, every 50 leads you generate on LinkedIn (or elsewhere), you'll want to convert ten leads into sales appointments. As you connect with people on LinkedIn and engage in conversation, invite people who are ideal prospects to have a sales conversation with you and keep going until ten people say yes. Of course, we're not going to call it a 'Sales appointment' so stick with me, and I'll explain.

With these numbers, you are looking at a ratio of 50:10:2. This means 50 leads converting into ten appointments and two sales. The size of your business and the volume you sell will determine how you set these numbers. 50:10:2 is a high starting point though and will give you something to aim for. You'll, of course, want to set the timeframe according to your business and how much you work in and on your business.

Set Sales Targets That Are Right for You

For example, a business with a team responsible for sales will likely want to set 50:10:2 as a weekly target for each person. For an expert-entrepreneur selling their time for money, monthly might be more appropriate. And if you're still working a full-time job, looking to transition to working part-time or full-time within your business, then quarterly might work best for you.

The sooner you integrate these measures into your business, the more natural things will be. A quick look at your diary will tell you if you are on or off track with your sales target. If there are too few sales appointments, go back to LinkedIn and look for connections that, with a little interaction, will have a prospect welcome a phone conversation with you.

In the next chapter section, we're going to be looking at exactly how to structure this conversation and how you present it to your prospect, so they happily jump on the phone with you.

Exercise

Before moving on to the next chapter, why not take a moment to consider how you will apply the content.

Within your industry, what problem do you solve?

When you think of doing sales calls with prospective clients, what feelings come up for you? What are your biggest concerns?

Based on your current circumstances, what will be your timeframe for booking sales appointments?

Key Takeaways:

- Generating leads via LinkedIn requires us to be clear on our intention for being on the platform; to book sales appointments with our ideal clients.

- Outright selling on LinkedIn is the quickest way to lose the respect and interest of your network; instead, we need to share content that positions us as an Expert in our industry.

- When we share helpful content that talks about the problem we solve, the symptoms of the problem and consequences of not solving it, we create our own audience.

- Inviting a prospect to speak to us about their problem and providing tailored advice is vital if we want to win new clients; the conversation is as much for us as it is for them.

- Giving good, honest advice – even if it means turning a prospect down or sending them to our 'competitor' - is the best way to quickly get known; when someone understands what we offer and why, they are better able to articulate the value we provide and refer other people.

- The best time to pitch our services is when our prospect invites to because they can see the value of what we offer.

Build a
Sales Process

2. Build a Sales Process

A sales process maps out the path someone will take as they progress from being a Prospect to a Client. It is a set of repeatable steps that you (or your sales team) will take with each new prospect that comes to your business. It goes hand in hand with the measures we discussed in the last chapter.

However, since our businesses are time-sensitive, we want to automate as much of the sales process as possible. By the time a prospect gets in touch, we want them to have already completed the majority of their buying decision. This way, we will win more clients in less time. We do this by creating a product ecosystem and a content strategy to surround it.

What are you selling?

One of the biggest reasons an Expert Entrepreneur will lose a sale is because they don't have clear products. If you look at an established business, there is always a clear product available. This might be a tangible item or a service. There is literature surrounding it and terms and conditions. When you call the company, the product is clear, with little to no room to negotiate. Everyone inside the company is clear about what they are selling and what they are delivering.

Within our business, we need to achieve the same level of clarity. When getting started, it is easy to fall into the trap of offering bespoke services for each new prospect based on what we think they need. Not only does this increase the time it takes for you to win each new client, but it also makes it harder for the prospect to buy.

When we don't have a clear product to offer, we don't have any literature for our prospects to look at. This means that when we pitch our services to our prospect, we'll need to follow up with a written proposal, which will take you time. In some instances, a bespoke proposal will be needed, but for the majority of your sales, and especially for those semi-interested, we don't have time to waste writing personalised proposals that won't lead to a sale and may not get read.

"People get busy, and they get distracted. The more time that passes... the higher the chance you'll lose the sale."

People get busy, and they get distracted. The more time that passes between the moment a person first realises they have a problem and agrees to solve it, the higher the chance we'll lose the sale. Often this won't be because our competitor gave them a better price or solution. They'll just revert back to being OK with how things are and living with the status quo. Other problems will spring up and distract them and feel more of a priority than the problem we helped them realise they had. Thus, all our excellent work will come to nothing.

Thus, we need to be clear about the product we are offering and make sure that it is easy to communicate and that it is repeatable. This way, we can create a brochure and website that helps our prospect to understand what we are offering and consider it. When we pitch our services verbally, we can invite our prospect to review our webpage (if we're speaking on the phone) or flick through the brochure while we pitch (if in person).

This level of clarity goes a long way. Interestingly, when a prospect says "I'll think about it" what they are saying is that they don't understand. It doesn't feel attractive or valuable to them. It is the ultimate 'fob off' that helps them to get out of the conversation quickly because they aren't saying Yes or No to you. If your solution doesn't resonate with them or doesn't feel tangible enough to understand, they'll likely say "I'll think about it" to get out of the conversation.

You may also find people say "OK, sounds interesting. Do you think you could send me an email to summarise that?" What they are saying is they need to see it visually to be able to consider it.

In these instances, having a webpage or PDF version of your brochure is a good idea as you can simply send it over to them without the need to invest time writing a proposal or an hour perfecting an email to send with it. It might feel tempting to do, especially if you want to work with this person, but remember, as Expert Entrepreneurs, our businesses are time-sensitive, and we simply can't afford to invest our time and take that gamble. Plus, attaching a brochure or directing a person to a webpage inspires confidence in your buyer that this is an established product and something you do regularly which ultimately increases their trust in you and the likelihood of them buying.

Create a Transformational Product

A transformational product is a promise to take your client from where they are now to where they need to get to. When we have this in our arsenal, our business becomes more efficient and easier to run because it is repeatable. By taking the time to identify recognisable milestones that each of our clients' needs to pass through to get a result, we can perfect our methodology and build content around it. Every time we undergo a transformation for a client, we refine it further, building in more content and value, and more mastery. For each successful transformation, we have evidence of our results and a story to tell our next prospect.

Ultimately, products give us something to build upon.

"Products should be transformational and therefore, inspirational. They should take a client from where they are now to where they want to be."

Creating milestones for our product gives it form and a basis to build our methodology; a methodology that is uniquely yours and therefore an asset to your business. Milestones also help our prospect understand what to expect if they work with us, and where they are in their transformational journey.

You don't need a sales page to launch a new product...

When I was developing my coaching product, I first pitched it over the phone. I had been delivering LinkedIn Profile Reviews for three and a half years at this point and writing LinkedIn Profiles in my own business for almost eighteen months.

I knew I had something to offer, so I pitched it to the next person I felt it was right for, which happened to be the day after I'd had the idea. I didn't have anything written down at this point so just pitched it verbally. My prospect was very interested in what I was offering and asked to see a website about it.

Being street smart at this point in my business journey, I knew exactly what this meant - he needed to see it summarised in written form to be able to make a decision. This didn't mean that I jumped to it and wrote a new sales page for it, this would be to invest a lot of time into an untested product.

Instead, I simply said "Actually, this is brand new I don't have it on a webpage yet, but I understand why you're asking. I tell you what, I'll send you an email outlining the package". This email won me the sale and was copy-pasted several more times in the next week as I continued pitching.

Once I knew I had something to offer, and several people had bought it, I invested time writing proper sales copy and created a new webpage on my site.

They also communicate to our clients that we know what we are doing, and that we're not just making it up as we go along.

A clear product will not only save us time but also brain space since we aren't reinventing the wheel every day. We can create sales pages and a brochure to match. We can develop documentation, worksheets and videos to help our clients achieve their transformation faster, all of which builds trust with our prospect. Further down the line, as we gather more evidence and add more features to our core product, we'll be able to justify increasing our prices.

"A clear product will not only save us time but also brain space since we aren't reinventing the wheel every day."

Administratively, you'll also be able to build time-saving processes to speed up the time it takes to process new sales. With my core product, there is a lot to set up for each new client, e.g. initial invoice, repeat invoices, online membership to the online course, Google Drive folder with uploaded content, personalised business planner, an initial welcome email summarising what I am sending them and a calendar invite for their first session.

Setting this up could take up to an hour, and if I get distracted, lead to mistakes. Since I repeat this process frequently, I have identified the steps involved and ordered them in the most logical way possible to save time and reduce errors. I simply follow the steps, and it saves me so much brainpower as I don't have to sit there, scratching my head, thinking about what I am doing. I simply follow the steps.

I store the steps in a free project management tool that I highly recommend (www.Asana.com). In it, I have a task set up that lists all the steps as separate tasks that allows me to tick them off once completed. The template also includes videos recorded on Loom (www.UseLoom.com) showing how to complete the task. This is great for me, as I so frequently forget how to do things.

When I take on a new client, I simply take the task labelled 'Template' and copy it, renaming it for my client and follow the steps. Each time I complete it, I review the order of the tasks and whether they are the most efficient way of doing things. Having repeated the task many times, it now takes me 20-minutes to complete the job compared to the previous one-hour it was taking.

If I expand the business and ask a member of staff to do it, I also know they have everything needed to complete the process without having to ask me questions. I will also know they are doing it in the most logical and time-saving way (something I am always motivated to know is happening). I don't do it often enough to justify building software around it, but I have automated it as much as possible.

(Please note, I didn't sit at my desk for hours perfecting it before getting my first client, or spend hours perfecting it once I'd proven the need for it by winning a volume of clients. Instead, each time I win a new sale, I ran the process and updated it as I go).

Products Help People Buy

As I previously mentioned, our prospect will complete 57% of their buying journey online before they speak to us. Outlining our products and packages is a vital part of helping our prospect with their buying decision.

The reality is, a prospect will not reach out to us unless they are confident that they like what we are offering and can see themselves purchasing it. Products allow our prospect to consider our solution, and how it fits with them, in their own time. It also means that, when you reach the Pitch part of your sales conversation, there are no surprises. The sales call simply becomes a chemistry check to make sure you're compatible and that they have correctly diagnosed their problem, and you are the right person to help.

"It's important to recognise that people don't like saying 'no' to people, or putting themselves in awkward positions."

It's important to recognise that people don't like saying 'no' to people or putting themselves in awkward positions. This is why the internet has changed everything because it has given people the option to find out what they need to know about you before getting touch. The power is now with the buyer and not with the seller. If we don't outline our packages and they don't sound interesting, a brand-new prospect researching online is unlikely to get in touch.

If we don't supply this information, there is a high chance that our prospect will return to their search and google our competitor. People want answers immediately, and Google gives them the option to get them. They want to conclude their search, either by finding the answers on your site or by continuing their research elsewhere. If they are just starting their journey and becoming aware that they may have a problem that needs solving, they may simply not continue to investigate it, and we'll lose a potential new prospect.

"If we don't supply this information, there is a high chance that our prospect will return to their search and google our competitor."

As a minimum, we'll want to include our packages on our LinkedIn Profile. The best place and only place, for them, is in the Experience entry for our company on our profile. If you don't have a website yet or you have to pay your web developer for each small adjustment, LinkedIn provides the perfect place to try the packages out before investing in the website. (It's important to note that LinkedIn is like having a stall at a street market with a huge footfall of potential customers, whereas a website is more like turning your bedroom wall into an art gallery and trying to get potential customers to visit when the only painting at the exhibition is your CV).

NAOMI-ROSE EVERLY

LinkedIn is like having a stall at a street market with a huge footfall of potential customers.

A website is like turning your bedroom wall into an art gallery and trying to get potential customers to visit when the only painting is your CV

Getting people to visit your website is hard work, especially if a prospect doesn't yet know they have a problem they need you to solve).

By outlining our services, we make our business more accessible, thereby getting closer to the promise of having clients come to us pre-sold and ready to buy. This is why we want to outline our packages and services on our LinkedIn profile (as a minimum). If someone likes the sound of working with us, we want to give them an idea of what working with us might look like so that, if they can see themselves working within those packages, they are confident when getting in touch. Without this, we'll find prospects not getting in touch, or if they do, they'll be unable to make a confident decision about working with you because this will be the first time they've had the opportunity to consider if your method and approach are what they want to do. A conversation where a person has already had time to consider working with us has more potential.

When a prospect just has questions, it makes it harder for us to establish their need for our product and justify our price. Without helping our prospect understand their problem and the extent of it, any amount we suggest will feel expensive. We want to avoid conversations where people are merely fact-finding. Instead, we need to engage the prospect in a hearty conversation where they've carved out dedicated time to explore the problem with us.

When we don't outline our products, potential prospects may opt to not get in touch at all. Several times, I've landed on the LinkedIn profile of someone I don't know and become instantly intrigued by them and the problem they solve. The problem they've outlined has resonated with me, and I can see that what they have described is something I need a solution for. Only, if I get in touch, what am I potentially signing myself up for?

That might seem obvious; I should send them an invitation to connect, but what do I say? What am I asking for? What if they don't help businesses like mine? This level of ambiguity is often too much for people, and instead of spending time crafting the perfect message that will save them from embarrassment, they simply don't send a message at all.

Outlining our products allows people to get an understanding as to whether they are someone we'd consider working with and if there is something worth talking about. It is easier to message someone and say 'I was on your profile and saw that you [insert product] and I wondered if we could have a chat' than to try to draft something clever.

As we move forward, we'll discuss how you can make it even more enticing for a prospect to reach out, and more comfortable for you to transform a new connection into a sales appointment with just one message.

One thing we should never underestimate is how shy people are, or you could say—motivated to avoid awkward situations.

Have you ever walked into a sandwich shop and immediately been greeted with "What can I get you?" before you've had a chance to have a look? If you're confident and not afraid of saying 'no' to someone, you'll feel comfortable having a quick look and deciding that you don't like the look of it and leaving. However, if you're even the least bit shy, or as I've said, motivated to avoid awkward situations, you're likely to stand there looking for a while before trying to navigate a hasty exit when the server isn't looking.

"One thing we should never underestimate is how shy people are, or you could say— motivated to avoid awkward situations."

If you do decide you want to buy something, the question "What can I get you?" is still hanging and requires an answer. For some people, it can be too much pressure. With so many options, conflicting taste buds, and the need not to hold anyone up, the pressure to make a decision could lead us to make the wrong decision or have a less than pleasant experience.

A great sandwich shop is all about timing — the friendly welcome and the availability of the counter person when you've had time to decide.

The same is true for our customers. As confident as we might be, we have to appreciate that others aren't and accommodate. A prospect may not want to phone us up for a single piece of information just to say "Nope, that's all, thanks. Just the one question." This is easy to do if you're calling a big company, but if you know the person - or feel like you know them from spending time with them online - there is little chance we'll do this.

We'll want to explain ourselves, get into a conversation, build rapport, talk about the people we have in common and then get to our point. It's not a good use of time for your prospect, and especially not for you if the question could have been answered online. We want to avoid prospects calling you out of the blue and interrupting your day, and instead, have them book a full diagnostic session with you using an online calendar booking tool so when you do speak, you'll be giving them your full attention.

"A sales conversation needs a clear beginning and end, and a clear objective that allows you to retain control of the conversation."

As we'll note later, off the cuff conversations seldom lead to sales. A sales conversation needs a clear beginning and end, and a clear objective that allows you to retain control of the conversation. They need to be scheduled.

Another vital thing to note is that most people's research takes place at night. If a prospect can't find the information they want, they will have to wait until business hours to contact you or receive your reply. A prospect will either have to delay their buying decision until they can speak to you or do what most of us do and google the answer, increasing the chances of them finding another supplier.

The new supplier may not answer the question either, but now your prospect now has two potential suppliers to call, not just you. A scenario best avoided. If they do delay and decide to call you the next day, we have to rely on them remembering, finding a moment to call you and 'feeling like it'. We also run the risk of not being available when they call.

This scenario is frequently played out in the independent beauty industry where appointments usually are made directly with the technician who delivers the treatments. For most customers, it means a delayed response and having to wait a long period before gaining any idea if the person can help.

As an example of how to resolve this, is a therapist near me who outlines all of her packages, including duration and price on a booking system. This allows me to book and pay for my appointment. When I discovered her, it was a Sunday night. Her website was the third I'd look at that night as I was motivated to release tension in my neck that was causing headaches. I landed on her site, saw the price, description and duration of services and booked an appointment for the next morning at 9 am.

Without the booking system, I wouldn't have been able to access this appointment as it was for 9 am the next day, on a Monday morning. I may have called later in the day, but she may not have been available, and we could have played phone tag for a few days during which time I could easily have found someone else. Instead, Leslie's booking system allowed her to earn in an hour what, otherwise, would have gone unsold and avoid wasting time messaging back and forth with a potential client.

For the expert entrepreneur, we want our prospects to complete the 57% of a buying decision online and move to the next stage. Online booking tools are fantastic for this as they allow our prospect to compare their diary to ours and book a sales appointment at a time that suits them, at the moment they are motivated to take action.

"It's about establishing products in just the right way so that our prospect can journey through our sales process effortlessly."

In my previous company, this is exactly what happened. A prospect interested in LinkedIn training for his team began googling the topic late at night. In his search, he arrived on my LinkedIn profile and those of my colleagues. Seeing my profile and my offer to deliver a company-wide LinkedIn profile review, he clicked the link and booked an appointment with me for the next morning at 11 am. The prospect went on to become one of our biggest corporate clients who not only purchased a substantial amount of services from us but also introduced us to the whole company and distribution partners. Making it easy for interested prospects to get in touch with us is an integral part of the process.

As we'll see as we delve further into products, a sales appointment is also a product, and this is what we mean by a Product Ecosystem. It's about establishing products in just the right way so that our prospect can journey through our sales process effortlessly, and only the right prospects, the ones that are pre-sold and ready to buy, get access to us - the time-sensitive Expert Entrepreneur.

Setting Your Price

Getting your pricing right is essential. As you pitch it to your prospects and the product develops, you'll get a feel for how much you should be charging by how easily people say yes to your price. To begin with, you might start charging what you feel comfortable with and what you might pay for a similar service. However, as more people say Yes to you, it is a good idea to raise your price. It is an excellent way to test pricing and your comfort with it when you haven't got much to lose. If lots of people are saying Yes, and you're meeting your income target, you can afford to lose a few clients because you priced the product too high.

I had my own experience of this a few months back. Almost at full capacity and not bothered if I took on another client or not, I increased my rate by 50%. To my surprise, everyone said yes, even listing the price as affordable and not something that would get in the way of them buying. I am very sure that my previous three sales, remembering their tone of voice in response to the price, would have paid my higher price had I set it at the time.

No matter what price you start at, you need to feel reasonably comfortable because if you don't believe in yourself, no one else will. When I raised the price of a LinkedIn Profile by £100 in my second year of business, I spent three months pitching the full price and quickly following it with 'friendly discount', putting the price back to where it was initially. Then, all of a sudden, something changed. I pitched the price and didn't offer a discount. The first prospect this happened with unusually pushed me to give a discount based on our shared business

Characteristics of a good product:

- Delivers a transformation. It takes a client from where they are now to where they want to get to.

- Focuses on results, not on hours of service or use of materials.

- Has a clear beginning and end, that is agreed and can be measured.

- Is replicable and easy to present in a brochure and on a website.

- Has milestones that form the basis of our methodology and provides flexibility to meet the unique challenges of different clients and perfect our approach.

- Starts with a foundation that, as more people buy, proves its value and evolves into a comprehensive package.

- Excites you and gives you new insights that can be turned into blog posts or include in your package.

- Is easy to talk about, especially when you have results to demonstrate what you do works.

- Helps you secure new business because it is easy to understand and easy for people to refer prospects to. A great product becomes a brand of its own.

community, which I'd previously stated was my reason for all discounts given. However, I flatly refused. Finally, I was seeing the value in my services and felt confident to ask for the money.

I know there will be a lot of industry mentors that won't agree with this advice, but personally, I am a fan of 'staying in your flow'. It is better to get started feeling good than not get off the starting blocks because you're feeling worried and anxious.

When setting our prices, a good rule of thumb is to create an hourly rate for our self, comparable to others in the industry and more than we would receive if we took a job within our area of expertise. With this hourly rate, we want to multiply it by the number of hours it will take to deliver our service and then add £1000. This calculation ensures that, as a minimum, we get paid a wage comparable to if we'd stayed in our jobs and that we're working for a profit.

The price we charge should mean that if we sell one package per month, our overheads are fully covered, and if we sell two packages per month, we're on our way to achieving our financial targets. With our 50:10:2 rule, we'll always be on track for achieving this.

Creating a Product Ecosystem

It's all very well setting our price point based on the above calculation, but how do you actually get someone to pay it? We can pack as much value as we like into the package and create a very compelling offer, but if our prospect doesn't yet trust us or subscribe to our philosophy, there is very little chance they will spend thousands of pounds on an unknown solution and someone they just met.

To win their business, we need to win their trust. We have to give people the option to spend time with us. This is why we give away free content. First, we give away content that adds value on our website and LinkedIn Profile and then content in exchange for an email address or phone number. (If you don't yet have a website, there is no need to rush. LinkedIn is the perfect midway point giving you great exposure with very little technical skill or investment required).

After a person has begun to spend time with us, we can offer them paid content in the form of an online course that offers a transformation. It won't be the full transformation they'd receive if they worked with us one-on-one, but it's a transformation that is compelling at the price we are pitching it at. Intrigued by our content, investing in our solution should seem like a natural and worthwhile thing to do.

Ideally, we want to create four different products: Gifts, Products for Prospects, Core Product and Product for Clients. Each of these products will be priced at a different level giving everyone in our marketplace a chance to access our content.

Our free content will speak to 100% of our marketplace and offer a level of transformation. This might be as simple as helping them define their problem and the extent of it or implementing a full solution. We can do this because not all problems are equal. If a company has a small problem, or the problem has a small impact, they won't want to be spending huge sums solving it, and we don't want to be the person they resent for taking all their money.

Product Ecosystem

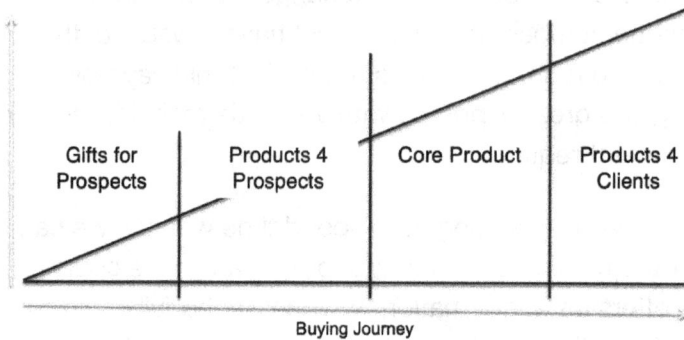

Reference: Daniel Priestley, Dent Global

What we do want is clients who are grateful for our services because their problem was significant enough to justify the price of the solution and they couldn't have solved it without us. We only want to work on projects where the client Is happy to be working with us and happy to pay our bill, and where the challenge is big enough to keep our interest and our skills at the cutting edge of the industry. The last thing we want is clients who later realise they really could have done the job themselves for a fraction of the price. We want our clients to be grateful we're there to help them because they recognise there is no way they could have done it for themselves. It is our job to help them work this out and make the right decision with them.

Thus, it doesn't matter if we give information away for free because if someone can solve the problem for themselves using this content, they wouldn't have been an ideal prospect anyway - and we need to know this before we invest time delivering a sales appointment.

What we want is the people who read our content and know they can't implement the solution themselves and come to us pre-sold and ready to buy. We want them to come to us and ask for a sales appointment (we'll discuss later how to name the meeting, so it is attractive to prospects).

When we give our information away for free, we're likely to be remembered. If we help a prospect solve a problem with free content, they'll likely tell other people about it. When the issue comes up in conversation, there is a good chance they'll share about their situation and what they did to solve it. They may give specific instructions based on what they have learned – from you – or refer to you as an expert they should work with.

If you've spent time with them on the phone explaining the solution and how it fits for them, they are even more likely to share insights and tips from your conversation, as well as explain your reasons for approaching the problem as you do. Inadvertently, they have just pitched you and your expertise on your behalf, and maybe better than any sales team could have done for you.

This is how we achieve word of mouth recommendations.

When we write content, we want it to speak to 100% of the marketplace because, ultimately, we only need two clients per month, and so, if 98% of visitors don't buy from us, it doesn't matter. We've got what we need.

Gift for Prospects

A gift is a product that is either free or very low priced. Just like other products, it needs to be transformational and deliver on its promise to take your prospect from where they are now to where they need to get to. In the early stages of a buying journey, something we'll discuss later, your prospect needs the opportunity to diagnose and understand their issue. Helping a prospect achieve this is transformational; it is helpful, it adds values, and the prospect will thank you for it.

Sometimes, the gift or low-price option is all the prospect will need. Your free product will help them to resolve their issue as it currently manifests or diagnose that this isn't actually the problem they have. Either way, we should be happy because it means we have added value to someone. A non-ideal prospect should leave our sales process at this point.

All is not lost, though. Hopefully, the information we have provided has been helpful and turned them into a mini-expert able to advise and point others with the same problem in the right direction.

If our information has been well received and seems appropriate to the situation, our mini expert will likely recommend us and our resources to their network, creating new prospects for us.

Our goal is to have non-ideal prospect disqualify themselves, so we save precious time and the disappointment of not achieving a sale. Getting this right gives us the best chance of achieving a high sales conversion, keeping our confidence high as well as our profitability.

Ultimately, we only want the right people to opt-in for sales appointments with us; those that have a real need and cannot fix it for themselves. As they read our information, we want our prospect to diagnose their issue further as well as come to an understanding of the impact of not solving it as soon as possible. We want our prospect to see the value of our services and the need to invest in our expertise.

Product for Prospects

It is possible for a prospect to digest our free gifts and jump straight into buying our high-ticket items; our core product. However, for the majority of your market, this won't be the case; they will want to do as much as possible to solve the problem and decide independently that they need to invest in a solution and a solution with you.

Again, this product needs to provide a transformation. It needs to take the prospect forward in some way, whether that is taking steps towards fixing the problem for themselves or further steps towards diagnosing it. The product also needs to complete the journey for prospects whose problem is not so acute by delivering some sort of transformation.

Ideally, we want to price our product between £47-£500. Having a seven in your price (£47) is kind of a magic number. Many years of research have gone into discovering that price tags with a seven in them are more effective than whole round numbers like £500.

Within the Product for Prospects margin, you may have several items at different price points depending on how much useful and transformative content you provide. Beginning to charge is essential, as we need to establish a buying relationship with our prospect. When we continually give content away for free, we are creating an expectation that all our content should always be free, making it hard to change the relationship later.

Converting long-time spectators, who have come to expect content from you for free, into paying clients is hard to do. We want to set the right tone for the relationship.

Core Product

A core product should follow all the rules we've outlined earlier. Where the other products solved small problems, like understanding more about their problem and a few hints on things to improve, your core product needs to solve big problems. It needs to be transformational. It needs to take them from where they are now, to where they need to get to.

This is where you perform your real magic. It is what you write case studies and testimonials about. It should be what the entire conversation, up to now, has been leading.

Our Core Product needs to under-promise but over-deliver. It needs to contain the essence of our company and leave people saying 'wow'. The promise you are making is to work with your client to deliver a transformational result, and sticking with it no matter the obstacles. It isn't priced by calculating your hourly rate, but rather by results. See later.

Product for Clients

More often than not, once you've solved a problem for a client, you'll be creating new ones. Products for Clients are services you offer or refer, designed to support your client after they have achieved their transformation. For example, a holiday consultant who books a family a holiday will now have created the problem of where they'll house the dog while they are away. A life coach who helps you to manifest a lottery win will now have a client that needs to learn how to invest their money. Products for clients may be an additional service you offer or something a partner organisation delivers.

Understand Your Timing

When starting our business, we want to avoid creating our Product for Prospects too soon. They can seem like an easy win because they can sell at volume, online, with little involvement from us after their creation.

The issue, though, is what it takes to sell at volume and how much you'll need to sell to breakeven. If we're an industry expert, it's unlike we have this skill – or the interest in it long term.

Without a strong mailing list or industry influence, we're unlikely to be sell high enough volumes to cover our living costs, and if we haven't yet perfected our Core Product, it is unlikely that our Product for Prospects will convert into sales of our big-ticket items.

To stay true to ourselves, we first need to perfect our Core Product by speaking to our target market and tweaking our offering until people in our existing network say yes.

Once we know exactly what we're, and we're positioned at the centre of our industry delivering transformational results, we can reverse engineer a Prospect's buying journey and create a Product for Prospects that aligns with our Core Product and converts prospects.

Spelling Out Your Packages

Outlining our packages on your website and LinkedIn Profile will give our prospects the confidence they need to reach out for a sales appointment. It allows a person time to consider if they can see themselves working with us in their own time at their own pace. This level of insight will give our prospect the clarity they need to feel confident booking a sales appointment with us because they already know they would like to buy.

> **"Outlining our packages on your website and LinkedIn Profile will give our prospects the confidence they need to reach out for a sales appointment."**

Having this knowledge before having a sales appointment will also help a prospect relax on the call and share with you the type of information you need to advise them correctly. It's important to note that, just because you call a sales appointment 'free', it doesn't mean it actually is. For your prospect, it is their time and their information they are handing over, and at this point in the conversation, this is a long way to being 'free'.

At the beginning of the sales appointment, they may be pre-sold on our lower-priced package, but the more we impress them on the phone and outline the extent of their problem, the more likely they will be to upsell themselves to our core product.

When we leave this information until later - as many teachers who sell from the stage or via webinars do - it only leads to regret because individuals have not been given the space and time to consider for themselves what they need and follow their intuition. Instead, they are met with price reductions and scarcity designed to make them feel they must act now or miss out and thus, they rush into the decision.

When we do this, we leave trust-building until after the sale, when the person is nervous and unsure, and this put us under far more pressure than if we just slowed down the process in the first place. Not only does the person feel uncertain about their purchase but they will also be unsure about you, which, if you're going to be working with them one-on-one for a while, could lead to problems.

"Under-promise and over-deliver."

As an Expert Entrepreneur working closely with our client to deliver a transformational result, we want to make sure our prospect is 100% confident in their decision and the journey they are about to undertake with us. This cannot be achieved via a webinar with a pressured sales presentation and significant discounting to 'buy now'. Those things work for selling information products and for experts (or semi-experts) who have diverted into marketing, but that isn't the Expert Entrepreneur. In time to come, we may choose to go down that route, but for now, let's build a strong foundation for our business first.

Note the stage at which I start calling our prospect a 'client'. A person only becomes a Client in our business after they have purchased our Core Product. This is because everything else up to now has been designed to get to this point. If people instantly buy our Core Product, we'd have no need for the other items in our Product Ecosystem.

For a prospect, we need to be aware that we still need to elicit permission from them to help further, and they haven't invited us fully into their lives to help them yet. If we aren't working with them one-on-one to deliver a transformation, then there is still more we could be doing. Calling them a prospect keeps us on our toes and our business growing.

Taking Our Prospect on a Journey

When developing our sales process, we need to consider the journey we are taking our prospect on. Ultimately, we want our most ideal prospects to make themselves known to us, and to create an opportunity for them to speak to us within the structure of a Sales Appointment.

Thus, all content should ideally conclude with a Call-to-Action (CTA); an offer or request that makes it easy for our prospect to take the next step with us. This might be to consume more content with us in exchange for an email address, or to take us up on a free diagnostic call: our sales appointment and our hook.

The diagnostic is our sales appointment; our chance to spend time with the prospect and help them understand the extent of their problem and whether they need to invest in a solution. A diagnostic sales appointment is one of the ten appointments we need each month to make up our 50:10:2.

In the early days of your business, we'll want to offer this call for free as we'll want as many people to speak to us as possible. As things grow and we become more well known, we may opt to charge for this appointment. We may also become pickier about who we speak to, to ensure that we're talking to ideal prospects and retain our target of two sales in every ten people we talk to. As time goes by, we'll get better at identifying who is an ideal prospect and who is not.

"A sales diagnostic call is essential to your business as, without it, you won't win any new clients. It is quite literally the bridge between wasting time and having a business."

A sales diagnostic call is essential to your business as, without it, you won't win any new clients. It is quite literally the bridge between wasting time and having a business, between being good at what you do and getting paid for it and being a confident business owner or fighting off the dark night of the soul.

It is also your chance to understand what is happening in the marketplace and how the industry is changing. By speaking to ten people each month, who are at the coalface with your marketplace, hearing about the problems they are facing on a daily basis, you will remain an expert in your industry able to deliver results.

We'll be able to speak with greater authority and insight. We'll be better able to match your solutions to their needs and write poignant content that resonates with your audience. Ultimately, we'll be an expert in our prospects' problems.

If we find that prospects come with the same questions and we're repeating ourselves, we may consider creating an item of content to help educate the prospect before the call. This will go a long way towards having our prospect come to us pre-sold and ready to buy and disqualifying non-ideal prospects.

It is also a good use of time as we'll be creating a valuable asset for the business that positions us as an Expert and supports the sales process. This type of content naturally creates our Gifts and Products for Prospects, and, most importantly, they come as a natural overflow of our main activities. They are in line with what the marketplace are asking for and therefore are attractive.

This is the magic I spoke of at the beginning of the book. It is the 20% study time that naturally turns into our sales and marketing. If we spend 10% of our time speaking to prospects and 10% of our time creating content that naturally overflows from these conversations, we are in flow.

Listening is the Key to Great Products

One of the most valuable things we can do in our business is to listen.

Listening gives us the insights and the feedback we need to create great products. The best thing we can do for our business is to get out and speak to our ideal prospects.

We don't have to have all our ducks lined up perfectly to start doing business. When I began TheProfile.Company, I certainly didn't have it all together. I only had my LinkedIn Profile writing service to offer, which was priced more as a Product for Prospects than an actual core product. It meant that I had to hit a high sales target each month, and things were much harder because of it.

"My business will tell me what it needs. If my business is my clients, my clients will tell me."

At the time, I didn't know what the core product should be or what my market would be willing to spend £2500 with me for (the starting price for a Core Product). However, the one thing I said was 'I don't have all the answers, but my business will tell me what it needs. If my business is my clients, my clients will tell me'.

Sure enough, as time went on, I began to see a common trend that all of my clients were struggling with that I knew I could solve and would enjoy solving. As I mentioned before, the first prospect I presented the solution to said 'yes'.

I didn't have a fancy webpage for it, or the details fully worked out product. All I had was a proposition. I pitched to my prospect over the phone and, when he asked me 'Where on your website is this?' I simply said it was new and that I'd send him an email outlining the what I was offering. I pitched the product several more times over the phone, improving the email I sent each time, and after a number of people brought it and I knew I had something valuable, I built a webpage and wrote a brochure for it.

When we are starting our business and approach our prospects this way, people trust us. They understand that we're new to our business and that we don't have everything perfectly aligned, but that they recognise we're good at what we do.

They recognise that we are passionate about what we do and have the skills to flex and bend to their situation and deliver a solution that is right for them and navigate any challenges as they arrive. And that we will stay committed until the outcome is achieved.

The key thing I want you to takeaway here is the message to just get started. Don't sit behind a computer making the perfect content, writing a training course, building an entire website, before you get out and make sales, as this is just an excuse for not getting out and meeting prospects.

Should I put my prices on my website?

When it comes to putting prices on your website, there are a few things to consider. If you have a high-priced product that is likely to turn people off, it is probably better not to put the price on the website but rather talk the decision through with the prospect first.

The value of what you do will be demonstrated through your sales call. It's important that you provide your prospect with the opportunity to explore their problem fully before opting out because of price.

Everything will feel expensive to a person if they haven't fully understood the extent of their problem and how much they need the solution.

That said, however, if you are receiving too many enquiries from people who can't afford your services, putting 'From £1450' on your literature will have non-ideal prospects disqualify themselves, leaving those who can afford your services continuing their journey with you. We'll discuss this more later.

Key Takeaways

- Our products need to deliver a transformation, taking our client from where they are now to where they need to get to. They need a clear beginning and a clear end with milestones marking progress.

- When a prospect can read about our packages prior to attending a sales call, they have an opportunity to consider what working with us might look like and whether it is something they'd like to do. They come pre-sold.

- Online appointment booking tools allows us to secure a sales appointment while a prospect is actively curious.

- Our main focus should be on creating our Core Product as this is where the transformation for our clients naturally happens.

- When we spend 10% of our time attending sales appointments, we naturally increase the likelihood of meeting our sales target.

- When we speak to our prospects, we learn about their industry and the problems they currently face. This helps us to create relevant and timely content, and a Product Ecosystem that answers pressing questions that means only the most ideal prospects book time with us.

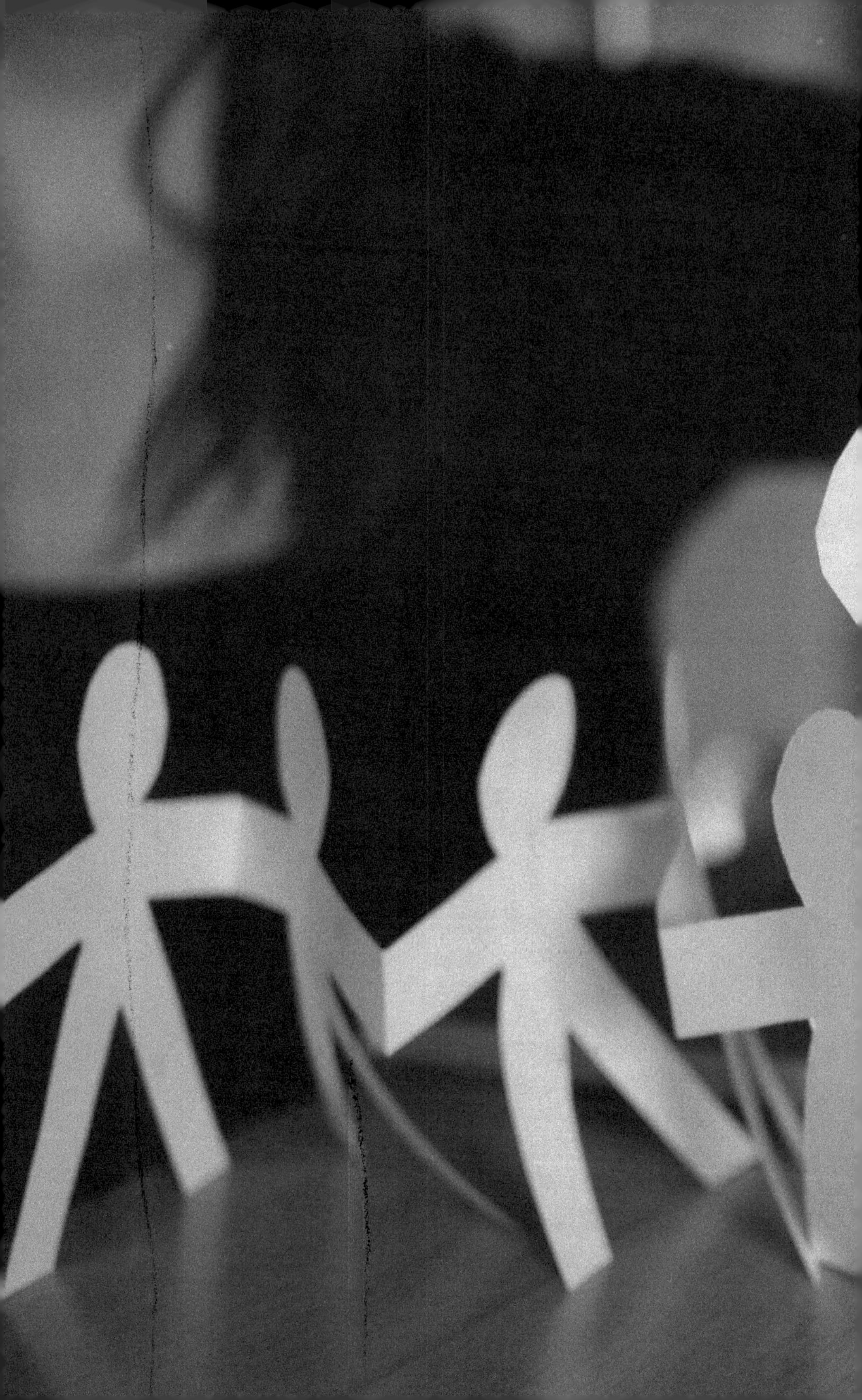

Design Your Sales Conversation

3. Design Your Sales Conversation

There are multiple ways to approach a sales appointment, and in the early days of your business (and as you build your confidence), you might want to consider your appointments as 'Research'. After all, that is what you're doing, and as we'll go on to see, the best sales approach is 'Consultative Sales'. This is where the call is carefully structured to allow the prospect plenty of time to explore their issues and identify the right solution for them. The days of hard selling are long gone, so if you don't like 'selling', don't worry—the Consultative Sales process is more like coaching.

With this in mind, it is important to note that we, as a service-based business, are time-sensitive. We have to be very clear how much time we can invest in a potential sale. Structuring our sales appointments is an integral part of this as we need to keep our conversations within an agreed time limit. Not just for our productivity and ability to earn within a limited amount of time, but also because we need to respect our prospects' time too.

With a structured sales conversation, we will be able to control the conversation and lead our prospect through each stage of the buying decision (see later), so they arrive at the end feeling empowered in their decision to either work with us or not.

When we package this conversation as a 'diagnostic' or 'review', it puts us in control of the conversation because it indicates an exchange. It isn't simply a conversation. When a prospect calls asking to learn about your product or messages you on LinkedIn, you have something to invite them to. You have the ability to invite them to a conversation that has a prescribed structure, where you are in control.

It gives you the ability to convert a casual conversation into a sales conversation, and it allows you to book conversations at a time that is convenient to you rather than accepting ad-hoc phone calls that interrupt your day. It means both parties are coming to a conversation ready to focus on the issue at hand. It also gives you the opportunity to ask for all decision-makers to attend the call.

As known experts in our industry, it can be easy to get caught up in conversations that, while enjoyable, are not leading us or our prospect, to the best outcome for them. It is also easy to find ourselves starting to solve problems for our clients and doing ourselves out of business.

It's also easy to find ourselves in a struggle with our prospect, sharing information and stories based on their objections and trying to convince the person they should work with us. Not only does this lose us power, but it is exhausting and extremely disrespectful to the other person.

Once, I was due to visit a friend several hours away. When I called to tell her I was on my way, she said she was about to go on a sales call and then she would do a few jobs around the house before I arrived. When I arrived two hours later, she was still on the phone, and I could tell

Be Careful Who You Listen To

When going out to market to pitch your services and obtain vital feedback, make sure you're actually speaking to the marketplace and not just other service providers. Several months back, a client came to me disgruntled because it seemed her target market weren't interested in what she had to offer. In fact, they had 'sniffed' at her ideal and told her it would never work. As someone
from her target market, I asked why.

It turned out that she hadn't been at a networking event with a cross section of her target audience, she'd actually been at an industry conference. The people she'd been speaking to were her competitors, people who had been in this industry a long time.

A lively conversation had followed with plenty of declarations as to why it would never work. All great feedback to be learned from.

But these people weren't her ideal market and they didn't know what the young, modern, tech-savvy marketplace wanted. The way they delivered their service was the way the service had always been delivered and they weren't looking to change it.

Thus, while hearing their rational was helpful, it was no indication for whether her marketplace would welcome her innovative approach or not. Thus, when pitching your ideas, make sure you're talking to the right people.

she wasn't preparing to get off the phone anytime soon. She wanted the sale and wasn't going to give up now that she'd invested two hours talking to this prospect trying to get them over the line.

Instead, I sat there and watched her try to close the deal. It was painful beyond belief. The prospect was clearly exploring something within her business, as my friend's questions had opened up space for her to thoroughly investigate her thoughts and feelings - and this was what she was now doing.

"A structured call allows us to transition through the vital parts of a buying process within a set timeframe."

However, it was clear that my friend wasn't listening. She was just looking for moments to interject and use what she'd heard to twist it to the outcome she wanted – buy this product. The call ended without a sale. My friend was exhausted, and her prospect had lost half her day to an unexpected phone call. Ultimately, everyone lost.

This is why structuring a sales call is so important.

A structured call allows us to transition through the vital parts of a buying process within a set timeframe. They enable us to elicit information from the prospect and help us determine whether we can help them and if we want to. They also provide an agreement as to what the conversation will be about, the value that will be exchanged and how long the conversation will go on for.

As it is a pre-booked call, the prospect will have carved out time for it and already considered the time spent is a useful allocation of time. They will come committed to the call and thankful afterwards for what was provided. When we cold call someone, this rarely happens as the person wasn't expecting the call and so we are just an inconvenient distraction.

What is a sales script?

We have a lot to cover in our sales appointment and not a lot of time to do it, so we need to make sure we structure the call just right, so we reach our conclusion on time. We also want to make sure we respected our prospects' natural buying process, so they feel able to make the right decision for them. We also need to make sure we elicit all the information we need to be able to make the right diagnostic of their situation and present the right solution.

To do this, we need to reverse engineer the call. We need to work out exactly what we need to know and exactly what the prospects need to see and hear to be able to make their decision. We need to craft just the right questions to achieve this outcome and build them into a script that flows naturally as a normal conversation.

Scripts are chunks of text that we say word-for-word on every call, or if not, word-for-word we at least convey the essence of, so nothing gets missed. Probably, the most important script is the introduction. The introduction sets up the call and lets the prospect know what to expect. It puts them at ease and, more importantly, lets the prospect know that we are taking control of the call.

Without this, it is easy to get railroaded into a conversation where we are responding and not eliciting the information we need. This creates a very strange dynamic between us and the prospect, which is unlikely to serve either of us well.

Client Story

Despite having her questions sorted, Tessa was nervous about speaking on the phone to her prospects. She didn't want to appear pushy with the sale, nor did she want it to appear she was asking questions from a script. She need not have worried, though. Tessa took the opportunity to book a call with another of my clients, Richard. She figured that, as he had had the same training as her, he would understand if she appeared to be a little robotic as she practised.

As it happened though, they had a fabulous call together, and they decided to work together. Cha-ching. Speaking honestly at the end of the call, Tessa asked for feedback on her script. It turned out Richard hadn't even realised it was scripted, despite being told from the outset. He felt the call flowed naturally and had simply been impressed how logical and well-structured it was. He fed back that it gave him the space to consider his situation and make an informed decision on whether to invest in a solution. It was a win all round.

One of the most important things we must do at the beginning of the call is to ask permission to inquire about their business and, if it is relevant at the end of the conversation, pitch your services.

By asking upfront, you give your prospect the option to find out more or feel comfortable saying no. With this all set out clearly at the beginning, selling will feel more natural and more like an ordinary conversation with a friend.

The secret is to add value. In doing so, not only will you demonstrate your expertise and the value of what you offer, but you'll also be creating a raving fan; a raving fan who, whether they buy from you or not, will tell others about you, building your reputation and exposure and ultimately bringing new prospects that come to you pre-sold.

Adding value in a sales call is easy to do when you're an expert. However, we've already mentioned about jumping ahead and doing ourselves out of business by going too far and solving the problem too early.

It is probably fair to say that this is more likely to happen in a coaching business where the power of one question can unlock a multitude of blockages for a client.

However, for the rest of us, this is very unlikely to be the case.

To have people want to book a 'sales appointment' with us, we need to offer something in return for their time. You might think that is a strange thing to say - 'in return for their time' - but the truth is, at this stage, it is *their time*, and until we build up the value with them, they only ever see the appointment as giving you their time.

> ## "To have people want to book a 'sales appointment' with you, you need to offer something in return for their time."

What we want is switch this dynamic, so a prospect is grateful to get the chance to speak to us and is receptive to what you have to say – and that they show up for the appointment. When we make the phone call a valuable exchange that focuses on helping a person either learn something interesting about themselves and the problem they have and moves them closer to solving it, people will want to show up for the appointment.

The perfect dynamic, and it's all in the exchange.

Your Sales Appointment Needs to Add Value

The best way to approach your sales calls is to offer some sort of diagnostic that gives feedback on how well they are doing or how critical their situation is. This will create an opportunity for you to demonstrate the quality of your advice in the context of their actual situation.

This is your hook.

In my LinkedIn Profile Review sessions, I provide all the answers my client needs, and I don't hold back. I open the call telling people that I am going to give them all lots of pointers that they are welcome to go away and do

Should you work with anyone?

The answer is no. In a service-based business, we need to protect our energy and our reputation. A sales call is as much for us as it is for our prospect because, before agreeing to the sales, we need to know that we can deliver - and that we can help and that we want to.

For me, 'actually helping' also translates into providing honest advice on whether their business is in the right place to justify investing in my LinkedIn Profile writing services.

If a business is not structured correctly, if they don't have clear products, a clear value proposition, or an enticing call to action (diagnostic call) that connects to their sales process, I will turn the prospect down because I know that, without these things, they will not be able to achieve a return on their investment with me.

I also know that I will struggle to write their profile. When a prospect comes to me without collateral (written brochures, blogs, product outlines – even if in draft), I know that writing the profile will take me much longer and impact my business. In these instances, I pitch to write their website and brochure first so we can explore the business before trying to fit it into a profile.

Providing honest advice sets us apart, but it also protects our business, and our other clients. If we're stressed out and overworked servicing one client, all our other clients suffer.

themselves, but if they would like to speak to me about how I can help, they are welcome to. I am here just to add value. This opens up a safe environment for my prospect to ask questions and obtain all the information they need to make an informed decision for them, and vice versa.

If a prospect feels that they can take my advice and implement it on their own, I am fine with that because I only want to work with people who know they aren't doing it for themselves, and want the approach I suggest.

I know my real value is in the implementation, not in the advice that people appreciate but typically don't implement. When I see someone has taken my advice and implemented it without my help, I feel good. I know that I have helped and that they'll likely recommend me to the next person they meet because they trust I'll look after that person and provide equally good value. When we operate like this, we have happy clients and a happy business.

We distinguish ourselves in the marketplace and get known. People talk about us. But more than that, because they have experienced our service and understood our advice and approach, they often go beyond just mentioning our name and passing our advice on, helping the prospect move closer to solving their problem. Intrigued by the insights that have been shared with them, and told that they came from us, the prospect is more likely to get in touch than if we were simply just a name.

Further, because this person has a better understanding of what we do and why, they are more likely to spot a prospect on our behalf and recommend us. For example, what if, at a networking event, a person who recently attended a diagnostic call with myself heard someone say, "I don't care about my LinkedIn Profile really, because my clients aren't on LinkedIn". Instead of just agreeing, my client said "I used to think that too, but then I spoke to Naomi Johnson (now Everly), and she pointed out to me that it isn't necessarily about your prospect finding your LinkedIn Profile, but rather the people who surround your prospect. If your profile speaks to your audience's pain, and the family and friends of your prospect know they are in pain and see your profile, they will recommend you and your profile to their loved one – and that is powerful".

Where once a person's objection to LinkedIn would have stayed an objection, and where once you may have chipped in and been dismissed because you're selling a product, now someone unrelated to your business and service is doing the work for you. They are breaking down objections and educating your marketplace on your behalf. Something which is absolutely priceless.

"As we add value, people remember us. They tell others, and we quickly get known as experts in our industry."

A real expert, in my opinion, is someone who is willing to provide honest advice and walk away from the sale if it isn't right for the prospect or for them; someone who is able to recommend a competitor even if the competitor wouldn't do the same for them; because they want a person to receive the best support even if it isn't them.

It takes a level of confidence and self-assurance in your business that, as you give, you also gain; that even if you are short on sales and needing the cash, doing the right thing by someone is still the right course of action.

Booking the Appointment

Of course, even with all the value that you're willing to provide, your prospect first needs to be willing to have an appointment with you, and this requires them to recognise they actually have a problem in the first place.

If no one is taking you up on the appointment, this is an indication that more work needs to be done in the marketplace to create awareness of the problem and the symptoms of the problem. We'll talk about this later when we investigate the stages of the buying journey.

If people are booking appointments but not showing up, this is an indication you haven't done enough to position yourself and the call as valuable in people's minds.

If you keep finding the wrong people are coming on the call with you, those who don't have authority to purchase, the budget or the need, then this again provides an indication of where to focus your attention.

If you find that your prospects need help and can afford your services but aren't purchasing, this is an indication that you're either pitching your product incorrectly or what you've created doesn't match their needs. This could also be the reason for price objections; however, price objections usually come down to perception.

Know Your Decision-Makers

Behind every prospect is a host of decision-makers. Even if the purchase is an independent choice, they still have friends and family that surround them that will have an opinion about their investment. Thus, your profile isn't just for your prospect but often for those who surround your prospect, such as a business partner, life partner, parent or even children.

With LinkedIn profiles ranking second in any name-based search in Google, you can be sure; if someone is researching you, your LinkedIn profile will be part of the mix. If your new prospect has invested all their savings with you, you want to make sure you show up looking your best and pitching the value of your services, or you could be putting your new client in a tricky position.

The person behind them who will want to know that the person they care about hasn't been cheated or made a poor investment. A profile, as with all your sales resources, must also speak to your prospect's support network, not just the prospect themselves.

"When booking sales appointments, it is essential to make sure you know who you are speaking to and whether there are other decision-makers in the mix."

When booking sales appointments, it is essential to make sure you know who you are speaking to and whether there are other decision-makers in the mix.

Recently, I provided 10-minute LinkedIn Profile Reviews at an Expo in London. After the show, a guy got in touch and asked for a further half-hour session. Recognising he was from a company with a small team, I made sure to ask who the decision-makers were and request they were on the call. When he told me "No, I'll take the information and pass it on", I knew this wasn't a sales call I should book, as there was no chance of it leading to a sale. I have plenty of free resources he could glean information from to pass on.

One way to overcome this is to record the call. If I know upfront or if I sense that other decision-makers are likely to need to sign off on the final decision, I will record the call and then ask the person I have spoken with to share it with the other decision-makers. I don't take the chance that they will be able to sell my services on my behalf by repeating my recommendations and reasoning for them.

In one such sales appointment last year, I provided a great deal of value within the call only to find at the end that the person had a business partner he had to run the information past. Knowing that it would be nearly impossible for him to repeat the strategy, I had laid out and the value I had demonstrated, I sent the recording of the call to him, telling him the exact minute within the 30-minute call that his partner should start listening.

I knew that this partner would be time-sensitive and not sit through 12 minutes of his business partner talking about what he already knew, but that he would listen for one minute, and if this one minute said something valuable, he would keep listening. Sure enough, the following week, having listened to the call, both business partners booked me to write their profile and provide ongoing training. Without the recording, I honestly believe this sale would never have happened.

Decision-makers are another excellent reason why we create products, as our prospect's supporters will want to know what they have brought, for how much and why. Leaving a prospect to explain what they brought on your behalf with no resources to back them up is going to put unnecessary stress and strain on them that will likely undo the sale.

Exercise

Before moving on to the next chapter, why not take a moment to consider how you will apply the content.

What value exchange could you offer as your Sales Appointment? And how long will the call last?
i.e. I offer a LinkedIn Profile Review

What will your prospect gain as result of coming to this session with you? And how will it help them move forward with solving their problem?

Who are the decision-makers typically involved in making a decision to buy a product like yours?

Online Booking Tools

Having an online booking tool is an essential tool for your business that you don't want to compromise on. There are many great tools available ranging in price that sync with your diary and can be connected to your Customer Relationship Management System and mailing list (should you have these).

Using a booking link will give your prospect the ability to book an appointment with you 24/7 and avoid the need for you to send suggested dates and time via email that expire if the person doesn't respond on time. They also allow the person to cancel at a click of a button making it easier for them to get in touch rather than just no show up. They can also rebook the appointment with just a few clicks, which again saves them time and makes it more likely you'll keep the prospect interested even if they couldn't attend the original appointment.

Tools you might look at include Calendly, Hubspot, OnceHub. It's worth Googling tools for the latest reviews and making sure the one you choose is compatible with your diary operating system.

Once a person has booked, you may like to send them an email series with helpful content that prepare them for the call. For this, you may need Zapier to connect your booking tool with your mailing list.

It is a good idea to only allow people to book a call within an allotted time. This will avoid people booking appointments that interrupt focused project time and having to shift your focus to sales multiple times a week. Organising sales appointments back to back creates momentum and mastery.

Key Takeaways

- A Sales Appointment needs to be an exchange of value and is as much for you as it is for your prospect. It is a chance to get to know each other and whether they have a problem you can and want to solve.

- If a prospect can implement this advice without us, we should let them. We only want to work with prospects who will value their investment with us because they couldn't have achieved the same results without us.

- Always be aware of those who influence your prospect and what they need to know about you in order to support your prospect in their decision to work with you.

- Having a sales script will put you in control of the conversation and ensure you cover everything you need to with the prospect within the allotted time, helping you and the prospect to make the right decision to move forward.

- If no one is booking a sales appointment/diagram with you, go back to the drawing board and delve deeper to find the pains your prospect need solving.

- Online booking tools are essential in time-sensitive businesses.

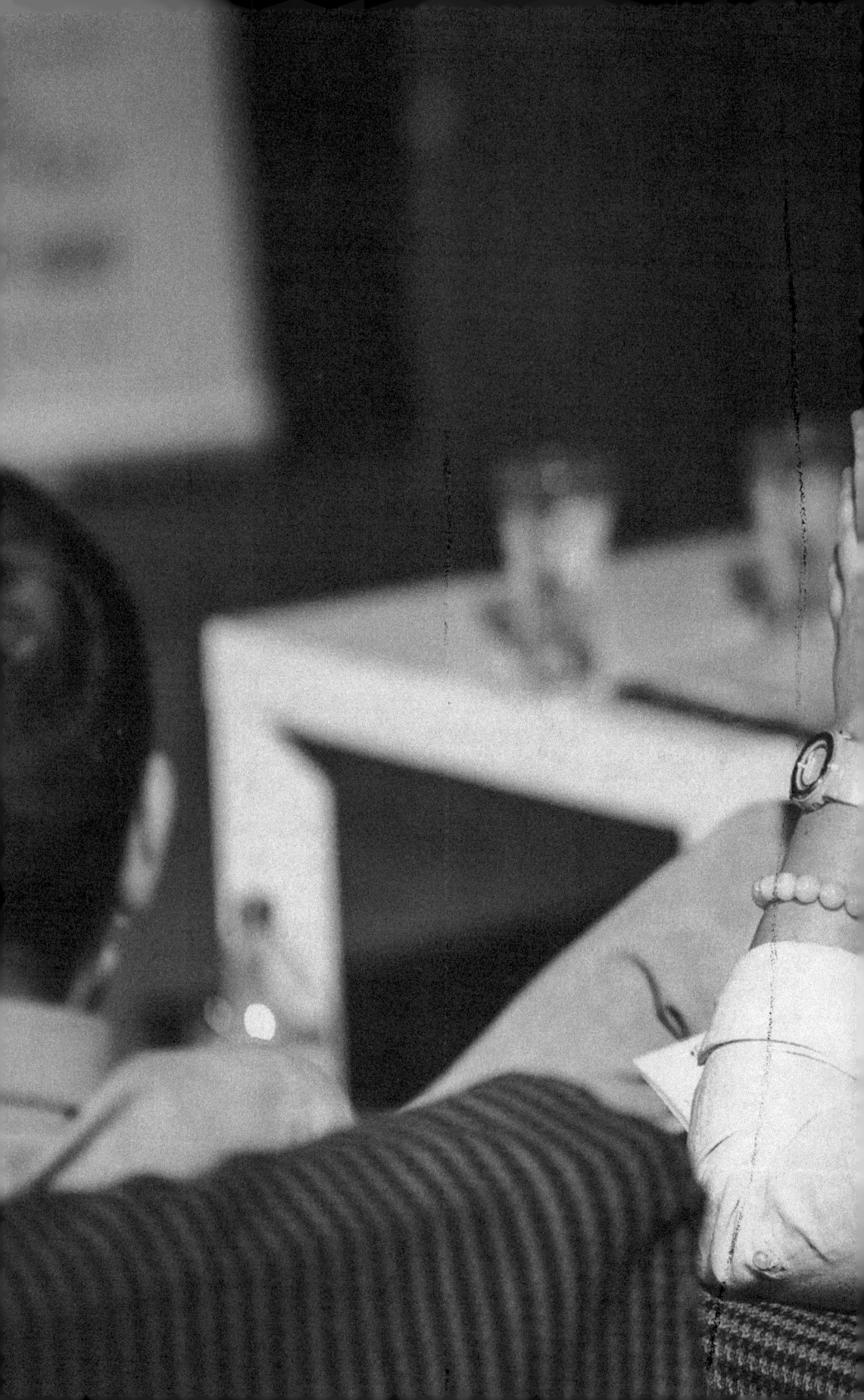

Master
Your Pitch

4. Master Your Pitch

The amount of interest you generate for your business is all in your pitch. If no one is asking to find out more about what you do, or if no one is asking you how much you charge, then you know you have a problem. In my experience, the most common response to a bad pitch is a confused look followed by 'So how do you get business?'. When someone asks you this question, it is usually because they don't get what you do, and thus how you could have clients.

Other clues also give you feedback on how you are being perceived. For example, prospects not showing up for a free consultation or diagnostic session with you is a good indicator that people don't value what you're offering. When people appreciate you and what you have to offer, they show up. If this is happening, you'll want to look at your messaging, the perceived value of your offer or your own personal brand.

A good pitch has people sit up and take notice. It stops people in their tracks and can turn a conversation from going rapidly downhill, to an involved and enthusiastic discussion.

It's all in the hook

If no one is booking sale appointments with you, it is usually for one of two reasons. Either no one needs your product or service, or no one *perceives* the need for your product or service. With the right hook, you can turn this around.

Recently, I've been receiving a lot of cold calls and speculative emails. It seems that somewhere I've managed to get my details on a list that is being sold. The first question the caller always asks is 'Could I please speak to the person in charge of....'

Immediately, my blood starts to boil because it only takes a few minutes to ascertain from my LinkedIn profile or my website, who would be in charge (and often if there would be a need at all for their service). The lack of research annoys me, and I usually let the person know it too. There is little chance they can sell to me.

However, the other day, I received a call from a national business who completely turned it around within 5 minutes. Having told him my annoyance that he didn't know my name, I asked him to say to me very quickly why he was calling. I was in the middle of something and not willing to change course, so I let him know this and said, 'Tell me quickly where you want this to go?'

What he offered me next was so compelling I would have been a fool to say no. I already knew this company, and I already knew the negative conversation on the street about their service, so with this and his cold-call approach, he was already on the back foot with me. Yet he turned me around with a great hook that instantly got me interested. He offered me a diagnostic that would reveal interesting information about my business that I didn't know and couldn't get anywhere else.

He acknowledged that I had let him know I was in the middle of something and he wouldn't continue to say too much now and instead asked if there was a better time to talk and sent me a meeting request.

Despite the bad start, he turned the call around by having a compelling hook that I couldn't turn down. I went on to buy from them. This is the power of a good pitch.

In this example, I didn't know that I needed the company's services or that I would ever need them, but I was curious about what their diagnostic would tell me. It is the same with the LinkedIn Profiles I offer. Most of the people I approach don't know that they need their LinkedIn profiles re-written, but they are curious to know what I will say about their profile.

Even if someone doesn't 'get' what we do or how our service will transform their business, a good hook will still have them show up for a sales call anyway. This is our opportunity to demonstrate what we do by applying it to their business.

The key is to make the hook very personal and very valuable. This way, even if they can't envision themselves ever investing money in your solution, they will still say 'yes' because they perceive the call as a big win from them. They aren't saying 'yes' out of courtesy or because they are afraid to say no. They will also show up for the call. You will know if the offer isn't compelling by the number of people that don't show up for the appointment and make no apology about it.

Pitching Your Value

When people value what you have to offer and value you as a provider, things go a lot smoother. Beyond having a compelling offer, people also have to perceive you as someone with advice worth listening too.

We've all been sold products that we've later regretted buying. We've all been sold products that we later realise weren't the right solution for the problem or weren't the right solution for us or were sold at the wrong time. Situations like this make us nervous about purchasing something new, and nervous about trusting the person we are speaking too.

"When we are willing to listen to our prospect and advise them correctly, and not just to serve our own need to make a sale, we do what is right. We stand out. We become a Trusted Advisor people talk about."

If we want to be an expert that stands out in our marketplace, and be someone that people are happy to refer, then we need to be someone that people can trust. And being someone that people can trust is about making sure we provide quality and timely advice that is right for them - even if it means we don't win the sale. Often, this will mean walking away from a deal we desperately need. It may also mean referring them to a competitor or similar service provider who is in a better position to help.

The sales appointment is our chance to shine. The questions we ask and the feedback we provide give us the opportunity to demonstrate our skills and the impact we can have on someone's life or business; we're confirming for the prospect that we know what we are talking about and are qualified to help.

We can increase a prospect's receptiveness to our advice and their enthusiasm for attending the sales call they've booked, by establishing a strong personal brand for ourselves, i.e. who we present ourselves to be.

One of my key tips for writing your LinkedIn profile is to tell your story within the experience section. Instead of writing about your job function, talk about the problems you solved and what you learned during your time working in this position that contributed to the approach you now take. A large part of our brand is our work experience, the exposure we have had to different situations and industries, the results we achieved and the insights we bring to the table because of them.

Our success as an expert isn't just about the product we are offering but who we are as a person because, ultimately, a client is going to have to interact with us to achieve the promised result.

If we have no track record to back up why we know what we do, people simply won't opt to hear our advice, or if they do, will question how you know what we do and if they feel it is valid.

Our LinkedIn profile provides the perfect opportunity to demonstrate how we have come to know what we do and why we approach problems the way we do. Telling the story not only builds rapport but also sells our prospect on our unique methodology and gives them more confidence to trust us when we work together.

> **"LinkedIn provides the perfect opportunity to demonstrate how you have come to know what you do and why you now take the approach you do with your services."**

The more someone understands this about you, the more they will consider you an expert in your industry and someone they 'know, like and trust'. The more they know, like and trust you, the more open they will be with their information during your diagnostic call and the more receptive they will be to your advice and the opportunity of working with you.

However, taking the time to write your profile well won't guarantee that someone will actually read it. If a profile is poorly formatted with varying lengths of text and capital letters in inappropriate places, it will create a negative impression instantly. If the profile is CV-based or your product is pitched poorly, it will do little to nothing for your personal brand, or for drawing people into wanting a sales appointment with you. Most people won't read it.

A carefully formatted profile, however, shows we've taken care with it and considered our brand and message carefully. It will go a long way to establishing our professional brand.

And it is your brand that will define how people will treat you.

Recently, I bought two pairs of trousers. One was for a very low price with a popular high street retailer. The other pair was from a more upmarket brand and four times the price. I treat the trousers very differently. I will garden, clean the house and take long walks in the forest in the cheap trousers, but I would never wear them to a business meeting. However, I will attend business meetings and events in my more expensive trousers, but once I am home, I will change out of them into the cheaper pair.

Why? Because I perceive the expensive ones to be more precious than the cheaper ones. I treat the trousers differently based on my perceived value of them. Even if I had received a discount on the expensive trousers and paid the same amount for both pairs, I would still treat them differently because of my perceived value of the brand. The interesting thing, though, is that the trousers may not differ that much in quality. It is merely the brand perception. It's how two stores have chosen to position themselves with the marketplace, and the customer base they are appealing to.

And it's the same with our own brand. If we want people to respect us and treat us well, we need to position ourselves carefully in the marketplace, so our target market interacts with us how we want them to.

Building Your Pitch

When we meet someone for the first time, we make a decision about that person within 0.3 seconds, and research from The University of Nottingham has now proven it takes eighteen 30-minute meetings to undo a negative impression. So, if we want to create a brand that stands out, that has people coming to us pre-sold and ready to listen, we need to be prepared with our pitch, so we make a good first impression.

However, in the early days of your business, you may not have a clear offering or understand the real value of the services you offer. As I've said before, one of the best ways to sharpen your senses and hone your business is to just get started.

But how do we do that if we don't yet know what we're offering?

At this point in our business, it is vital that we start pitching our services as this will give us the feedback we need to grow our offering and pivot the company if needed.

The way to do this is to be transparent. It's OK to tell people that we're "in development" and researching your ideas. When we do this, we'll find people are very receptive and willing to help.

They will be more than happy to take a diagnostic call with us and let us practice pitching our services. They will be patient if we get it wrong and happy to provide feedback to help us make it better. Bringing prospects into our business early and involving them in its development will give us access to great ideas, and likely create strong relationships that have people champion us to others and recommending us to ideal clients. When getting started, this type of validation is invaluable.

Plus, there is always the possibility that we'll convert the person we are speaking to into a client – why wouldn't we? They're an ideal client, we're capable of delivering the result, they are telling us how they'd like to solve the problem; and all we're doing right now is figuring out how to pitch it. It may take a more extended conversation, but if our prospect sees the value we bring, they are going to be forgiving about our pitch if they see they need our expertise.

When we take this approach, things become a lot easier. People won't expect us to have all the answers and so we'll have the space to grow and explore naturally, in our own time. A LinkedIn profile is great for this as it is easy to update and tweak as we refine our message. Plus, it is connected to all our new and existing business associates giving us vital free exposure.

What we don't want to do though is to show up confidently and loudly with one business one week, and then another the next week. This just leads to confusion and will create a negative brand image. Eventually, people will turn off and stop listening because they can't refer or hire us.

People who change their business proposition too frequently lose credibility and, with it, their 'Trusted Advisor' and 'Expert' status. Our prospects simply don't believe in us anymore.

A pitch is the answer you provide to the question 'what do you do?' Your pitch is the 60-seconds introduction you provide at networking events, your pitch is your LinkedIn profile, your pitch is your website, the purpose of each blog you post, each piece of content you post and how you show up in the world. It is the message that you stand for.

The Right Time to Launch

When I hear people say they want to start a business, I always tell them that the best time to start is when you see a problem in the world that needs solving, and you're absolutely adamant that it has to be solved your way because, when you are passionate about what you do and how you do it, you will be consistent.

We might mess up the delivery of our pitch or not yet have the clarity we need to pitch it well, but one thing is for sure, we won't undersell it or undersell our self.

When I began selling LinkedIn profiles for £400 each, I didn't have proof of concept. I didn't have plenty of examples proving the quality of my work. All I had was a massive belief in the reasons why a profile needed to be re-written and how it should be done. My new clients instantly picked up on this passion and believed me.

They bought my services because they trusted in the quality of the advice and recommendations I had given them, and took a chance.

NAOMI-ROSE EVERLY

The best time to build a business is when you see a problem in the world that needs fixing and are adamant it needs fixing your way

When we are passionate about what we do, we are consistent - even if *how* we pitch it changes daily. When we know what we stand for and the problem we solve, it doesn't matter how much we mess up the delivery of our pitch or vary it, we are still being consistent about the problem we are looking to solve.

We can tell stories that demonstrate our point. We can listen to our prospect's situation and happily volunteer information and insights that ensure people 'get it'. As we do this, we start to recognise what works and what doesn't. Eventually, our pitch develops, while at the same time building a fanbase and even winning new clients. As long as we are working on perfecting the pitch and structure our sales calls, we can forgive ourselves for not being perfect every time. At least, we're on our way.

Your Pitch is For Everyone

In an era of information overload, our brains are programmed to stereotype and pigeonhole people in a matter of seconds. This means that, if something is too hard to understand, we'll simply switch off. In a face-to-face situation, we have no choice but to keep listening and be polite. However, online, we can just 'swipe left' and leave the conversation.

The key to a good pitch is to craft it, so people want to keep listening and so everyone will understand us.

We want to avoid using jargon or sentences that only mean something to those who have the same level of education as us. The majority of your clients won't understand our expertise and the technical reasoning behind it. If they did, they wouldn't need you. What they need is the solution to the problem they have, whether they recognise they have a problem and need a solution, or whether they don't.

Therefore, your pitch needs to be relational. It needs to be something that people instantly 'get'. They need to 'get it' to the point where they either say 'I have that problem, tell me more' or they say, 'Oh my brother-in-law struggles with that, I'll have to introduce you'. Your Gran and your kid brother need to be able to understand it because it is only in a person's understanding of it that they can make referrals and talk about us.

You need to consider that everyone is your audience because you never know who you are talking to, or who they know. It's not that you're trying to sell to everyone, it is that you need to be understood by everyone so opportunities can find you.

When you speak to your prospects, you want to enlighten them. You want to leave something behind with them that gets lodged in their mind, an interesting fact or piece of information that is highly sticky, so that the next time a subject comes up in conversation, the person relays it and your name comes up.

Niching Has Changed

One of the questions I am frequently asked about is niching. Traditionally, niching has meant targeting a particular segment of the market, getting to know them very well and pitching to them.

DANIEL PRIESTLEY

You get what you pitch for,
and you're always pitching

However, since 2008, things have changed. Niching today is not about choosing a geographical location or demographic, but more about the problem you solve.

"Niching today is not about choosing a geographical location or demographic, but more about the problem you solve."

Recently, I took on a new client, and in our initial conversation, he told me about his software and the problem that it solved. The product has excellent scope to help a lot of businesses in many different fields. However, he then declared that he was going to niche the company to the transport industry. I immediately asked him why since he had no background or experience in that industry. He told me it was because it is essential to target a specific group and niche.

I told him I wholeheartedly agreed, especially since the scope for what he was offering was so large that any marketing materials would be at risk of being generic. However, I asked him to consider an important distinction. Targeting the Transport Industry is a campaign, but not a niche.

Niching into a particular industry requires a reason. People will want to know why. They will want to see we have an understanding of the industry and its challenges, and, to really make it work, we'll need a pre-existing network who can open doors for us. It's an "all-in" approach. The reason we provide has to have clout. It can't just be because it seemed like a good opportunity or a marketing strategy.

The reverse of this, however, is to create a niche by focusing on the problem that you solve and the industries and people who need you to solve that problem. From here, we can tailor marketing activities to create a focused campaign targeted at a particular industry.

The difference is that we aren't professing to know one industry better than another, nor are we cutting off options to work with other industries. Our credibility lies in our ability to solve the problem, not within the target demographic of a niche we know little about.

When we are expert at solving a problem, all we need to do is demonstrate that we can solve it. It's up to the buyer to decide whether they trust us to apply our theory to their industry. If we are credible at what we do, we will be able to provide a good answer when asked: "how will this apply to my industry?"

Leading with the problem we solve not only gets our markets attention, but it will also start to define our audience naturally.

For example, I specialise in LinkedIn Profiles. I don't specialise in LinkedIn Advertising, nor do I need to. I also don't write profiles for job hunters or students. I write them for Entrepreneurs and sales teams who are passionate about making a difference in the world and want to become known as experts in their industry and build a thriving business.

What I don't do is target a particular industry like technology, retail or consulting. I write profiles for a broad spectrum of industries and do so easily because my specialism is on solving a problem; how to pitch a service and have prospects come to you pre-sold and ready to buy. The principles I apply work across all industries allowing me to interview many fascinating people and learn about lots of different industries.

My niche isn't therefore limited to a small specialist group of people, like the transport industry, but rather to the problem I solve. The problem I solve narrows my marketplace down, as only a particular type of person has this problem to solve.

If, at any point, I decide I want to work with a specific group of people, say Coaches, I can run a campaign to that group of people with messaging tailored just for them.

"What we want to do is be clear on the problem we solve, and then run targeted campaigns to types of people or businesses."

People visiting your LinkedIn profile could be coming from any background or industry. To capture someone's interest so they read it, you need to appear relevant. You don't want an ideal prospect to read your profile and think 'That's interesting to me, but they specialise in this industry. They don't want to talk to me' and then click away.

There are, of course, businesses that do tailor their solution to just one industry and position its leaders as experts in that industry. If we make enough noise, the question of 'why' will dissipate as our results will speak for themselves. However, I would caution here to check how big the marketplace really is and whether you have a strong enough passion for this group to fuel your enthusiasm for what it is going to take to achieve a result, as are you prepared to start turning down other clients so 80% of your clients end up being from only that industry? If the answer is yes, go for it.

But if the answer is no, as it is for me, then I would caution against it. It's something that requires a great deal of thought before committing.

Instead, what we want to do is be clear on the problem we solve, and then run targeted campaigns to types of people or businesses.

Match the Psychology of LinkedIn

On LinkedIn, we need to be aware of how people operate and how we capture and keep their attention. We need to write our profile to match the psychology of how someone operates on the platform.

One thing that must be noted is that no one cares about you on LinkedIn. That might sound like a harsh thing to say, but the truth is, until you become relevant to them, they don't care.

LinkedIn is a busy platform. People are usually 'on their way' somewhere. Either to find a person, post an update, or just pass a little time reading articles during their break.

If a profile reads like a CV, they won't read it as it is not relevant to them. They aren't a recruiter.

It's not rude. It's like walking down a busy street; you don't stop and try to get to know each person you pass, nor do you feel bad about it.

It's just the same on LinkedIn.

Therefore, we have to build it carefully. We need to quickly set the context of the conversation by outlining the problem we solve so we are quickly understood in the context of their world, so people want to read on. Each paragraph needs to lead naturally onto the next and create momentum. It needs to build rapport and replicate a real-life conversation as if the person is meeting us in real-time. Powerful sentences on LinkedIn start with 'I believe...' or 'In my experience...' because it reveals something within us and draws people into our world. It allows people to buy into us and our motivation.

We also need to anticipate a person's objections by answering their questions before they have even thought of them. We need to understand how our prospects buy and write to match their natural flow of thought.

Our profile is written for our ideal prospects and non-prospects, as the majority of people in our network are non-prospects. If we want them to introduce us to our ideal prospects, then we need to ignite an understanding within them about what we do.

LinkedIn Profile Example

One of my clients' LinkedIn profiles opens with:
"In today's world, the first sign of a heart attack is the heart attack. For the first time ever, it is predicted that parents will outlive their children. Fertility is on the decrease as miscarriages are on the increase. And our farming choices have led to our fruits and vegetables to contain just 5-20% of the nutritional value they did 100 years ago."

These facts are interesting and easy to remember. They are easy to interject into a conversation, and, in fact, if you were the person in the conversation volunteering this information, it would give you a sense of knowing what you're talking about. This type of information is practical and informative. Already, just in the opening paragraph we have learnt something. It has had an impact and isn't going to be forgotten. It is, however, going to make us want to read on and find out the solution.

This is the type of quick situational insights we want to share to demonstrate the importance of the problem we solve. It will pique people's curiosity and set the context for the conversation we're about to have within this LinkedIn profile. Just be careful not to provide too much information that it now appears like a lecture or text from a book that a person hasn't opted to read.

How You Show Up Sets the Tone

How you present yourself sets the tone for conversations and the results you achieve. Within a few weeks of updating Anthony Brown's profile, the CEO of a Hampshire-based Architecture firm, he noticed a dramatic change in the types of connections he was receiving and the conversations he was having. Previously, only recruiters approached him or people he'd met at networking events. After his profile was updated, Anthony began receiving connection requests from peers within his industry who wanted to discuss big ideas.

He was also approached by a young graduate who was looking for a firm that shared her values. She said she had researched lots of local companies and upon finding Anthony's profile, requested an interview stating that she believed in his values and why they were also important to her. Anthony wasn't recruiting nor had he even considered it, but having been approached by someone who was an exceptional fit for his business, he hired her.

Nick Cusack, a Licensed Insolvency Practitioner, also noticed a dramatic change in the types of conversations he was having with new connections and their understanding of the value he provides. He reported that conversations with new connections tended to be far more advanced and trusting after his profile was re-written because the prospect didn't feel they were talking to a stranger but someone they already knew they trusted.

A LinkedIn profile, as well as how you pitch on your website and other materials, shows how well you know your business and how much you respect your prospect's time. When pitched correctly, it tells people how to engage with you and about what. It positions you as a leader within your industry and someone easy to refer.

It establishes you as an Expert.

Exercise

Before moving on to the next chapter, why not take a moment to consider how you will apply the content.

Outline your key philosophy for solving your client's problem, and why you are adamant your approach is the right one?

List key experiences and moments in your career that shaped this philosophy

List the reasons why you are an expert in this area

Key Takeaways

- People don't attend Sales Appointments, but they do attend a nicely packaged conversation where they gain further clarity on the problem they are experiencing or about themselves.

- You just need to get started. If say you're still developing your ideas and offering, people will accept this – provide excellent insights and advise into your industry to demonstrate your value.

- There is a high chance that those you practice your pitch and sales script with will buy from you. Remember they aren't buying you for being great at sales, but for being great at solving the problem you specialise in.

- Your LinkedIn profile is your window to the world; how you show up sets the tone for how people will treat you and respect you within your business.

- Use your past experience entries on your LinkedIn profile to tell the story of how you became an expert and how you developed your philosophy and perspective. Your target audience isn't recruiters and doesn't want to read a CV.

- When you lead with the problem you solve, it not only gets your audience's attention, but it also starts to define your audience naturally. You avoid the need to niche into a particular market and risk alienating groups of potential customers.

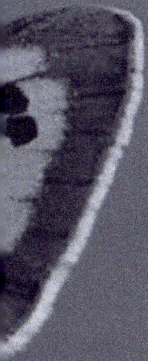

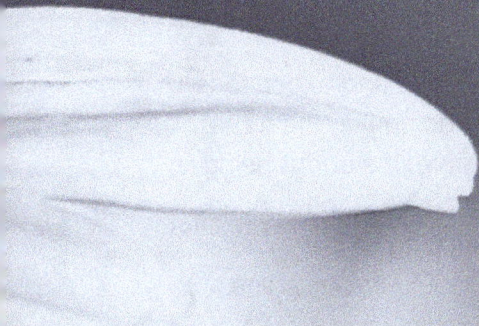

Finding
Your Value

5. Finding Your Value

Being an Expert isn't about building your ego or promoting yourself as something you're not. It's not about having all the knowledge and information, and always knowing the answers. It is also not about reading a few books and becoming a self-professed expert, as some influencers would have us believe.

Being an expert is about knowing how to carefully navigate our prospect from where they are now to where they need to get to while anticipating potential challenges and handling obstacles like a pro.

It's about bringing your expert knowledge and experience to a situation to solve a problem and doing it in the most efficient and cost-effective way possible. It's about being able to anticipate challenges and successfully navigating the ones you couldn't foresee and sticking with the situation until you bring the client over the finishing line.

That's not to say we will know how to handle every situation or that we can predict what the outcome will be, but it is about having plenty of life experience to draw on to make the best decisions in the heat of the moment.

Ultimately, though, it's about having your client say thank you for transforming their situation because they couldn't have done it for themselves.

What really makes an expert?

The internet is littered with people from every industry claiming to be experts within their industry. Some are. They have the track record. They have spent years perfecting their skills and the scars to prove it. Others, unfortunately, are just influencers; people who have posted content and quickly established a following online. Some of their advice might be good, and some of it might be bad.

For the audience learning from the influence, it's impossible to decipher whether their advice and insights are credible or not. It would take a genuine expert to review the content to tell us if the advice is actually correct.

"Being an expert is ultimately about having your client say thank you because you did for them what they couldn't do for themselves."

In many respects, this gives everyone a licence to start their own channels and say what they like; after all, who is going to check? However, if you are going to build a business around your expertise, your value must go beyond the ability to create content and build a social media following.

Your value is in your ability to deliver transformational results for your clients. Results people talk about. Results that people will pay for.

This isn't claiming you're an expert because you achieved something once, like publishing a book, and people began asking how you did it, so you opened a business to show them. This will just lead to people making the same mistakes as you and missing out on real industry advice from people who have professional industry experience.

Instead, it is about having real industry experience in all aspects of a project and knowing with absolute confidence how each element comes together to create the finished whole.

It also isn't about achieving a result in one industry and then thinking your advice applies to every other company on the planet. It also isn't about knowing how to put something together mechanically and making it functional.

Rather, it is about being able to achieve a result multiple times in multiple industries and in multiple ways. It's also about having failed, as often we learn the most from our failures. It's about having worked around experts in a variety of different fields that surround our speciality, and understanding how they all fit together. And it's about understanding why they fit together the way they do and seeing the bigger picture.

I am frequently approached by prospective clients who have previously worked with a marketing team who've put together a sales campaign for them, and I am always to be shocked at what they have created.

While it functions mechanically, it seems little thought has gone put into the content and how the product is pitched. We might be able to see a home page, sign up for a mailing list and receive five emails back, but none of that matters if the words used aren't pitching the product effectively and attracting the right target audience.

Although a person can put a marketing campaign together technically, this doesn't mean they have the expertise required to deliver a complete solution capable of delivering a result.

The real value of any company or expert is one who knows the extent of their expertise and when to bring in other professionals to help complete the big picture. Professing to know more than we do, and not understanding our own limitations will only lead to disappointed clients and a compromised reputation.

Why Create Content?

Today, the internet is flooded with help and support for just about anything you want to achieve, and for the most part, it is free. For the majority of your marketplace, this might be all that they need. The free information can answer their questions and give them the transformation they need.

However, for our prospects, this won't be enough.

For us to build a thriving business, we want to attract our most ideal prospects, those that have a real need for our services and the budget to pay for it, i.e. those who have a juicy project we want to get our teeth into. Projects that challenge us and keep us on our toes. Projects that keep us at the coalface and the forefront of our industry, growing our skills and helping us retain our expert status.

To achieve this, we don't want to be taking on any project that comes along. Instead, we want to make sure we're investing our time working on the right projects.

Giving away free content is a great way to create an audience and become known as the 'go-to' expert within our industry, but it is also a great way to filter out the prospects who don't have a real need for our services.

If a prospect can answer their own questions and solve their challenges using free content, they don't need us. Knowing this before we invest time providing a diagnostic sales call will save us a great deal of time and unnecessary rejection.

"When creating content, speak to 100% of your audience because you only need 2% to purchase from you."

The prospects we want to attract are those with significant problems that cannot be fixed with free content. These are the clients who need help and are willing to pay for it. People that are so grateful to us for helping them that they feel indebted and to want to help us in any way they can in return, all while forgetting they paid a healthy sum of money for us to solve their problem in the first place. This is the definition of a happy client and the type we want to pursue.

Since we have a limited capacity and only need to take on a few clients per month, we don't need to worry about the big, wide marketplace: just those who have a need right now and the budget to invest.

Therefore, it doesn't matter how much free advice we give away because we only need a small percentage of our marketplace to want to work with us at any given time.

Giving free information and advice will not only help position us as the 'go-to' expert, but it will also build rapport with our audience and help ensure that when our topic comes up so does our name. Free content will satisfy the needs of those in our audience with small problems that don't need to hire someone to help them, while helping our most ideal prospects come to the conclusion, independently of speaking to us one-on-one, that they need to invest in a solution, and we are the expert to help them.

The benefits of free content are far-reaching, but we mustn't let that distract us from the art of winning new business and delivering transformational results.

Are You an Expert?

If you sell a service and the promise to solve a problem for your clients, then there is a high chance you're an Expert Entrepreneur. You're likely someone who has spent years mastering your knowledge and capabilities and have a unique take on things.

You see a problem in the world that needs fixing, and you're adamant it needs fixing your way, so much so that you've put everything on the line to strike out on your own and become a solo-entrepreneur.

Definition of an Expert Entrepreneur

If you sell a service and the promise to solve a problem for your clients, then there is a high chance you're an Expert Entrepreneur. You're likely someone who has spent years mastering your knowledge and capabilities and have a unique take on things.

You see a problem in the world that needs fixing and are adamant it needs fixing your way. So much so that you've put everything on the line to strike out on your own and become a solo-entrepreneur.

Your main product is you, your expertise and your ability to solve your client's problems. You're good at it and you create transformational results that people talk about. If you could, you'd spend all day working with your clients, researching your subject and talking about it. It gets you out of bed in the morning.

Your main product is you, your expertise, and your ability to solve your client's problems. You're good at it, and you create transformative results that people talk about. If you could, you'd spend all day working with your clients, researching your subject and talking about it. It gets you out of bed in the morning.

For some people reading the above, you might be starting to question whether you are an expert and if this book is right for you. If you are, hold tight. You are very likely to be underestimating and downplaying your own experience and what you have to offer.

If you've read this far, you must be a person looking to build their own business selling your expertise, which means you already recognise you have something to offer and are now trying to work out exactly how to do it. You are an expert. You're an Expert Entrepreneur because you've branched out alone to start your own business selling your expertise.

Becoming an Expert?

The general opinion is that if you spend 30-minutes a day researching your topic, within seven years, you'll be an expert. When I first heard this, I went into a panic. I looked at my schedule and tried to make time each day to read and study so I could eventually become an expert in something.

However, the regime never lasted. It felt more like a chore, and it wasn't like there was a set syllabus with an essay or test at the end. I soon became demotivated and stopped following the schedule.

Or did I? Becoming an expert is actually about following the path of least resistance and doing what comes naturally to you. For most people, they probably haven't even realised they have become an expert. They have just been doing what they enjoy doing, reading books, watching videos, making notes talking to people and, in most cases, building a career in the process.

Over a ten-year period, I attended copious amounts of training courses during the week, over weekends and read tons of books on my subject. From my estimations looking back, I was investing at least five times heavier in my development than my peers who relied on their employers to identify their training needs and pay for it.

I was investing all my money in new training courses and testing my learnings in my own business and with clients. Since it was my own business and I was at the coalface of my industry, I was trying out new things, succeeding and failing and working out what to do and what not to do, without even appearing to 'try', I cultivated my expertise. It didn't feel like trying because it came naturally. It was what I wanted to do, and I enjoyed it.

"Our expertise is always found on the path of least resistance."

A true expert is someone who has a natural inclination towards their subject. They have prioritised the subject ahead of any other and invest personal time and funds developing their knowledge and experience. It might not be their full-time job, but it is where their interests lie and where they want to spend their time.

With this person, you don't have to give them a motivational talk to switch off the TV; they just do it. They naturally keep themselves abreast of new industry developments and talk to others about their topic, especially those whom they can help. They would happily help someone solve the problem, and even if they won the lottery, they would want to continue working within their area of interest.

Follow the Cookie Crumbs

Steve Jobs, in his Stanford University Inauguration address, said it's not until you look back and follow the cookie trail that you start to realise how everything came together perfectly.

And in my experience, things always do come together perfectly.

When we take time to look back over our lives, we tend to see just how perfectly everything worked out. In the moments we feel overwhelmed, situations can feel so final, yet, when we look back over our lives with the right line of enquiry, it doesn't take much for us to see why things happened the way they did and to be grateful for them.

The truth is, every experience we've ever had, whether good or bad, has shaped us. Every success and every failing have helped form our opinions, points of view and perspective and made us the unique human being we are today. These situations have created our expertise and our resolve to branch out alone, put our lives at risk, and declare to the world that their problems should be solved our way, using our unique methodology.

It's how we've arrived where we are and why we do what we do. Often unknowingly.

Several weeks back, I was working on a LinkedIn profile when caught myself saying to myself "If I encode the message..." and stopped myself. 'Encode the message?' Why did I say that? That's a bizarre turn of phrase. With a little reflection, I realised that it was terminology I had learned at college, completing my Communications and Media qualification. Note, at this point, Mark Zuckerberg was a mere 12-year-old and social media, as we know it today, was still to be imagined.

It made me realise I didn't arrive at what I am doing today because of recent events and industry developments, but instead, I had started on this path long before. My interest and development in this subject began right out of school when I was picking my college subjects. My expertise had been in the making for over twenty-five years long before I could have imagined what I would be doing today.

Everything we do in our lives, and especially everything we've enjoyed and has come naturally to us, gives us clues and, as Steve Jobs said, provides a cookie trail.

It is only when we look back, we feel liberated. Suddenly, everything seems to make sense. It becomes easier to talk openly about our journey because every one of our mistakes has shaped us.

Every book we've read, movie we've watched, challenge we've faced, job we've had, every rejection and every door opened, all of them have crafted us into the unique individual we are and set you on a path to bring us to exactly where we are today.

> **"Someone who has a passion about their industry, who sees a problem in the world that needs solving, and someone who wants to stand up and solve it."**

Someone who has a passion about their industry, who sees a problem in the world that needs solving, and someone who wants to stand up and solve it. If you've read this far, I can only assume this is you, and you're ready to go for it.

Just Get Started

The good news is that you don't have to have a proven track record in solving the problem to get started. You just need someone to believe in you and give you your first opportunity to solve the problem. This might not be your full pay rate at the beginning, but if you're passionate about your solution and why it is the right one, it will become infectious. Others will see it and believe in you. They'll take a chance on you because they recognise you have something they don't, and you have enough enthusiasm to stick with the project and figure out what you don't know along the way.

As long as you leave a client in a far better position than you started, and you deliver value in excess of their investment (as perceived by the client), you'll have begun your journey as an Expert Entrepreneur.

Find the Jewels

When you start to see the cookie crumbs, you also begin to see the synchronicities and patterns in your life and how you've been preparing for this role your entire life. When we look at things this way, it becomes easier to see our own value.

There is a beautiful saying "A butterfly cannot see its own wings". During our lives, we become so familiar with ourselves and what we 'do' that we often cannot see our unique value and our contribution to different situations.

Asking people how they see us is an important exercise as it will often provide an insight into us that we wouldn't have been able to see by ourselves.

Taking time out to explore our past and reveal the synchronicities in our journey is an essential step to uncovering our value and what we now bring to a situation as an Expert Entrepreneur. Often, we can be so forward-facing, so determined to move forward and make our current goals work, that we fail to look back and reveal all the jewels in our journey that give us our credentials today.

Understanding our journey isn't just about building our sense of self-worth and confidence. When we understand our journey, we are better able to articulate stories and share case studies and bring alive the possibilities for our clients and prospects.

The stories we tell and the examples we give can help our clients to understand what we do and why they need us. They instil confidence and hope that our solution will relieve their situation, and they too can get similar results.

Building Your Confidence

The more you show up and help your audience, the more you'll grow in your confidence and understanding of why you are an Expert. The key thing is just to get started. There is always someone out there in need of your help, and you never know when or who will benefit from a video or blog you have posted, nor when they might get in touch.

Your stories, examples and case studies make fabulous content that can help prospects relate to you and understand the extent of your expertise.

Several years ago, I won a new client simply from tweeting a quote. The person saw the quote and became intrigued. She began following me on social media and read lots of my content. By the time she reached out to me, she was already sold on the idea of working with me.

I've also been at networking events where people have told me they had a problem with their LinkedIn account, and they managed to fix it thanks to a video or blog on my website.

A butterfly cannot see its own wings

It is little conversations like this that let you know you're making an impact, even with people you have never met. A great way to start understanding your value is to begin blogging because you'll soon realise just how much you know. Writing content helps you to think through your points of view, and as you articulate your message, you'll begin to see why you know what you know, and that, actually, it's a unique perspective you bring because of the journey you've been on.

It also has the added benefit of being read by your target audience. And not everyone has to like it. Our content, our perspective and point of view, might not be everyone's cup of tea, but that's OK. As we said before, we create our content to help 100% of the marketplace, but it is only 2% of the market that we actually want to work one-on-one with. We don't need everyone to like us.

All that matters is that we're getting results for our clients. As long as we are doing this, it doesn't matter if someone disagrees with our point of view because it's clear that our point of view gets results. And that's all that matters.

Exercise

Before moving on to the next chapter, why not take a
moment to consider how you will apply the content.

**Interview 5-10 from your network and ask them how
they see you. What do they see is unique about
you? What do you contribute to a situation? How do
they perceive or rate your skills?**

**What would an exciting juicy project look like to
you?**

**Who could you approach right now with your
solution, that may buy from you? Or provide
valuable insight into your product offering?**

Key Takeaways

- Being an expert is about having your clients thank you for helping them do something they couldn't have done without you.

- Your life has prepared you for this moment. Every challenge, every success, every choice you've made has uniquely prepared you for this moment.

- Take the time to look for the cookie trail to understand your unique value and what you bring to a situation.

- Begin writing content because, as you do, you'll start to realise how much you know.

- Write content that aims to help 100% of your marketplace because you are looking for the 2% who can't solve the problem without you and are happy to invest in your solution.

- Ask people to help you understand and articulate your value, as it is almost impossible to do yourself.

- Articulate and pitch your value through case studies and examples, to help your prospects understand and appreciate how you can help them.

- You may never know the impact your content is having, and who is benefiting from your content.

Become a
Trusted Advisor

6. Become a Trusted Advisor

Now you recognise why you're an expert and have begun to pitch your services clearly; it is now time to take it up a notch and get noticed.

One of the key things to note about an 'expert' is that, at their essence, they are a Trusted Advisor. Someone who can provide timely insight and advice and help you make the right decision for you.

We've already mentioned that an expert is not about ego but adding value. They come in service to help their prospect make the right decision for them. Often, this means to educate the prospect or provide industry insights and even to teach a prospect how to buy.

Recently, I visited an outdoor shop to buy a raincoat. There was a 40% sale on, and I selected two jackets that I liked. To my eyes, the only difference between them was that one was black and the other was purple. I was naturally drawn to purple as it is my favourite colour, only the purple one was £40 more expensive and to pay this much more money just because of its colour, I needed an explanation. I examined the tickets on each and other than the wording being slightly different, and I couldn't make out what was different about them. I've never brought proper raincoat for hiking purposes before and so I didn't know what to look for.

I decided to ask an assistant, but he couldn't help. I called a friend, but he didn't know the answer either. I was completely stumped. I had no idea how to make my decision. Eventually, I concluded that the first shop assistant was a trainee and spotted someone who seemed to have more authority. I walked up to him and said 'I have no idea why these two are different prices. I want to make the right investment. Could you please teach me how to buy a jacket?'

"One of the key things to note about an 'expert' is that, at their essence, they are a Trusted Advisor. Someone who can provide timely insight and advice and help you make the right decision for you."

On the surface, this was probably a strange question not often heard on Tottenham Court Road in London on a Saturday afternoon, but it was a real one, and one we are all asking every day whether we know it or not. It is also the reason Google has become an intrinsic part of the buying process for nearly all of us when buying just about anything.

The conversation with the sales guy wasn't that useful, only to the extent of leading me to buy the more expensive jacket. It was something about it being windproof (and being purple) that helped me to see the added value in the more expensive jacket. However, as an inexperienced buyer, I knew I had a need, I had the budget, and the timing was critical. I was tired, just wanted to go home, and I knew I had to get an answer because I needed a jacket.

If you were a specialist in outdoor gear and wanted to build a loyal following, this would have been your moment to shine.

I didn't know how to make the right decision; I didn't know how to evaluate between different products. I needed someone to educate me to the point where I could make the right decision for myself, and also feel good about my decision.

This is the power of a Trusted Advisor.

When we are ill-equipped to make a decision, we are probably making the wrong decision. Or if we are making the right decision, we won't know it because we're too uneducated to know it; we don't feel confident in our decision, and therefore we worry about it.

A few years ago, I began to migrate my computer files to an online backup service. I researched a few services and opted for one that seemed right. This was when the product was relatively new, so there weren't that many options available. I wasn't confident I was doing it right or that it was right for my needs. I was always worried about my files, and if I had myself covered in case something went wrong. I worried about it a lot, and eventually, I took a trip to the Apple Store so a 'Genius' could take a look and help me get the right solution.

It turned out I had the best backup process available. The genius told me the service I had was more sophisticated than the one he had, and that he was impressed. All that worry had been for nothing. Though it turned out years later when I moved to Google that all my folders and files were empty and everything was gone, but that's another story.

When we are providing our services, we want to have happy clients who are confident in their choice to work with us. If a client isn't confident, it can lead to friction within the relationship that is hard to pinpoint. Instead of being open and receptive to your ideas and suggestions, they are prickly or defensive, or closed-minded. If the relationship started well and seemed positive when they agreed to purchase from you, but has now changed, this could well be the reason.

"The more someone spends time with you and develops their trust in you, the stronger the relationship will be."

Feeling good about our buying decision is essential. As the above story illustrates, it isn't just at the point of sale that a client needs to feel confident; it is also in the weeks that follow.

The more someone spends time with you and develops their trust in you, the stronger the relationship will be.

Zero Moment of Truth

Research by Google has proven that a person will not buy from a company during their first touchpoint, i.e. the first time they hear of you or visit your site. Instead, it takes 11 touchpoints in 4 locations over 7 hours.

A touchpoint could be your brochure, leaflet, website, or meeting you, for example. The location could be one or two of the Social Media platforms, an email or in-person. However a prospect discovers you, research suggests a person needs to spend an average of 7 hours with you before they will feel ready to buy from you.

As small business owners with limited time, I think we can agree that 7 hours per prospect one at a time is impossible if we're to make our business profitable. As we've already discussed, our businesses are time-sensitive and therefore, our objective needs to be to cultivate prospects using online content and automated processes, so only the right prospects get in touch. And when they do, they come to us pre-sold and ready to buy.

By using online tools to publish content, we are able to replicate the stages of the buying journey and accumulate the 7 hours we need our prospect to spend with us without investing any additional time beyond creating the content. At this point, you may not even be aware that your prospect is engaging with your content.

Using the Tools

The key thing is to supply the right information in the right way according to where the prospect is within their buying journey—something we'll discuss in the next chapter.

When We Fail to Build Trust

Some years ago, I managed to back my life into a corner, and I desperately needed help to navigate my way out of it. I expressed my concerns at a networking event, and the lovely lady I was speaking to pointed out a life coach in the room she felt could help. She introduced us, and I made an appointment to talk to him.

I had so much anguish within me; I couldn't wait to meet him. As soon as we sat down for coffee, I launched into my problem, and he confirmed he could help. We negotiated a price and set a date for our first session, but our first session absolutely bombed. He knew, and I knew it.

During the session, I found it hard to open up or take on board any of his recommendations. I was a nightmare client from beginning to end, and I didn't like it. After the session, I reflected on what I had been feeling and why.

When we came to our next session, it was clear he had done the same. He began to address it by asking me a few questions, but I knew where he was going and had come armed with my answer, so I asked permission to share it.

It turned out that the reason I had been so awful was that I didn't trust him, but worse than that, I didn't know him. I recognised that during our first meeting I had only spoken about myself, desperate for him to present himself as my saviour. I had invested every penny I had into this coaching programme, and I was nervous. And now even more so because I didn't know anything about him, who he really was, what his credentials were, or his method and philosophy. Simply put, I didn't trust him. He was still a stranger to me.

To overcome this, we ended up spending the entire session talking about him. By the end of it, I was happy to continue and went on to achieve the promised end-result faster and to a higher level than he imagined I would. It turned into a successful coaching relationship.

And it taught me a powerful lesson. When there is no trust, there is no relationship, and there are vital stages within the buying decision that cannot be omitted.

With all the free tools available to us, there are no barriers to entry. Anyone, even as young as 13-year-old, with a laptop and a passion can create content and position themself as an expert in their field.

When it comes to marketing our business, things have never been so easy. When I started in business in 2006, we only had email and mobile phones to communicate. Unless you had a new and expensive digital camera, recording a video meant recording to tape and taking it to a shop to be converted on to a DVD. Once you had the DVD, the content needed extracting onto the computer and was usually so large it would crash the computer. Editing equipment was also expensive and hard to access as a new start-up. It was so time-consuming and such a faff that very few projects could ever be finished.

Today, the tools available to us are second to none, and they are free. If we don't know how to work them, there are plenty of tutorials available online to help. We really have no excuse.

If you're brand new to your business, LinkedIn will replace the need for a website, and give you the flexibility to tweak and test your message until you hit gold. Videos can be recorded and edited on your phones and uploaded directly to YouTube, Facebook and LinkedIn. Gaining exposure to your business is easier than ever.

Building Your Presence

As we've already mentioned, pitching our message well and consistently is imperative, especially when building our presence and getting known.

The key is to start creating content that people want. Now that we've identified the problem we solve for people, we need to uncover the questions our prospect is asking and create content that answers them. We can learn what people are asking by posting questions on social media, reading comments on other people's content, as well as searching keyword databases online.

Reading articles is also a great way to get the juices flowing. We may read things you agree with or things we disagree with, but it doesn't matter. Reading articles can create inspiration for our own content by writing on the same topic but with a different spin. We may find an article and be inspired to write our own article going into more detail, or more detail on a particular aspect of it.

"Now that we've identified the problem we solve for people, we need to uncover the questions our prospect is asking and create content that answers them."

The more we show up in the marketplace as a credible source of information solving real problems, the more people will want to tell their friends and family and introduce us to their network. As we create content, we'll be creating the 11 touchpoints Google's Zero Moment of Truth speaks about, and as we post it on different social media, we'll be creating our 4 locations. Eventually, we'll have enough content to give our prospect the opportunity to spend 7 hours with us.

As we begin to achieve this, we'll start finding prospects arriving in our sales funnel pre-sold and ready to do business with us. The moment is actually quite strange; before now, I've been prepared with my sales script and ready to go through the stages involved, only to have the person blow the conversation out of the water by asking 'how do I buy?' As we'll discuss later, the answer to this question is 'by letting me run my sales script with you', but the joy of knowing someone has already decided they know, like and trust you enough to be ready to buy, is a good feeling.

Add Value

When creating content, make sure it adds value. Give away more than you might expect and recognise that you can do this safely because your value lies in the implementation. As we said before, information is free these days, and if you're not publishing content about it, it is very likely someone else is.

By knowing your own value and what you have to offer, you can easily begin to identify where the line is between what you give away for free and what is charged. The choice is yours.

Personally, I know that I have a problem holding back information and advice. Therefore, I built it into my process to provide comprehensive LinkedIn Profile Reviews, where I tell the person everything. It saves me from having to strain myself and hold my tongue. My prospect is always grateful for the in-depth and honest insights, but the benefits go beyond just this phone call. Invariably, whether the person buys from me or not, they will tell others about me because they have been impressed and they trust me to help their friend in the same way. Thus, they actively recommend me and rate me highly, with a loyalty that doesn't give my competition a look in.

"Give away more than you might expect, and recognise that you can do this safely because your value lies in the implementation."

As well as providing in-depth advice, I also make sure to evaluate if it is right for my client to invest with me. If I can't see that they can justify the investment or it isn't the right time, I tell the person. I might want the business, but if it isn't right for the individual, I'd rather say so than have a client who becomes resentful of our work together when they realise for themselves it wasn't the right move.

A Trusted Advisor is always honest and adds value. They are never self-serving. Back in the 1990s, the British brand Kwit-Fit recognised this and became known as the brand that would always tell you if your car tyres didn't need changing. It won them much custom because many other companies were well known for bumping up your bill by recommending replacing tyres that didn't need to be.

Honest advice is refreshing, and it builds trust.

Be Remarkable

If you want to get people talking about you, you need to be remarkable. Not just at delivering your service, but also in how you interact with your prospects in person, on a sales call, or via your content. Great content will lead a person to want to spend time with you and book a sales diagnostic appointment. The more content they have digested before they speak to you, the more advanced the conversation will be, and more likely they will be to buy from you.

> **"The more you open the gates to your information and let people look around the store, the more you'll find people interested in working with you."**

Generally, people are wary of sales appointments because they haven't yet decided to buy (or buy from you). Saying 'no' can be awkward and difficult so most people won't volunteer themselves to go through this unless they really have to. A great way to get around this is to have a strong Call-To-Action; an offer people can't resist. This is the 'hook' we spoke of earlier.

The more you open the gates to your information and let people look around the store, the more you'll find people interested in working with you. As we said before, you only want the right people wanting to work with you, so it's OK if individuals take the information, apply it and get results. This is great because, without speaking to the

NAOMI JOHNSON —————

As an Expert Entrepreneur we want to be billing 70% of our time, investing 20% of our time studying to remain an expert in our industry and 10% of our time running our businesses.

The magic happens when your sales and marketing become a natural overflow of your study time prospect, we have disqualified them as 'not an ideal prospect', freeing up more of our time to talk to ideal prospects and continue to create great content.

Helping someone who isn't your ideal prospect to solve a problem is a great way to raise your profile and get known. The more people you help, the more referrals you'll receive. If someone has managed to solve their situation by digesting your free information, they are likely to tell other people about you.

"Helping someone who isn't your ideal prospect to solve a problem is a great way to raise your profile and get known."

Your name will come up in all the right conversations.

When we have problems, we generally seek out advice from our peers and, as humans, there is nothing we like better than to be the one to recommend the right solution. If you've helped a person to fix a problem and they trust you, your name will come up in conversation. They will recommend you. Unlike the person recommending, this new person may just be your ideal client with the time, need, budget, and authority to buy from you.

Building Your Content

When building our content, it is important to recognise that there is a science to what we share and when. In-depth information or too basic information can turn a prospect off. If they haven't yet decided whether they need our solution, offering an intensive 'how to' may not appeal to our prospect. Or if our prospect has decided they need your solution but need more information, we will turn the prospect off if they can't easily find more information to help them make this decision.

The same is true if we push our paid product on a prospect before they have had a chance to get to know us properly.

When building our content, we want to approach it carefully and make sure it fits with the natural buying journey of our prospects. Asking someone to purchase too soon puts us at risk. If they feel forced into buying something before the relationship is strong enough, it'll put the relationship on risky ground. The prospect will continually be evaluating us and our service and whether they are getting value. What we don't want is nervous clients. Instead, we want confident clients that trust us to advise them properly and are confident in their decision to invest money with us.

We do this by understanding and respecting how people buy.

Key Takeaways

- A Trusted Advisor is someone who provides honest, in-depth, and timely advice that helps their prospect make the right purchasing decision for them.

- If the foundations of the relationship are not strong enough, you won't be able to ask for the business, or if you do win it, you may find the relationship compromised.

- Research by Google found that people need to spend 7 hours with our content, see us in 4 locations, and have 11 touchpoints with us before they are ready to buy.

- We want to create content that meets our prospect where they are at in their buying journey; providing details and facts is too advanced for someone who hasn't yet identified they actually have a problem to solve.

- The more you show up in the marketplace as a credible source of information, the more people will want to tell their friends and family about you, and introduce you to their network.

- Add value in all your interactions and give honest advice, even if that is to say they shouldn't work with you.

How
People Buy

7. How People Buy

Understanding how people buy makes everything in our business simpler as it will tell us where to invest our time. As we said from the outset of this book, our goal is to make sales, and sales require sales appointments. Thus, our first job is to inspire our prospect to want to speak to us, and our second is to support our prospect to make the right purchasing decision for them.

In our time-sensitive business, we want to use content to build our following and filtering out those who will never buy from us, so our most ideal clients come to us pre-sold.

The Internet Changed Everything

In our modern world, things have changed dramatically from what they once were. Research by LinkedIn and Almeratie group in 2012 showed that more than 57% of a buying decision is now made online before a prospect will consider speaking to a sales representative. This may sound like a made-up statistic or even out of date, but as we progress through this section, hopefully, you'll come to see just how, in your own purchasing, things have changed. Becoming aware of how you buy will help you to understand your prospects and create content to help them buy from you.

I remember when I was a child wanting to buy a hi-fi sound deck. You may remember them or at least seen them recently in the vintage cafes that now buy them second-hand. They were made up of various decks including a multi-tray CD player, record player, radio, tape deck, sound equalizer etc. All I knew at the time was that they looked good and I wanted one, and so did my brother. We were both as keen as each other to purchase one and saved all our money and did extra jobs around the house to earn money to have one. My brother created a chart to map his progress that went the full height of the wall.

"57% of a buying decision is now made online before a prospect is engaged a Sales Representative."

- LinkedIn and Ameratie Group

Every Saturday after my brother got through cleaning the house to earn his next instalment, we would beg our Dad to take us to the shop to see the hi-fis and test them out. We would spend hours with the salesperson going through all the details and playing with them. Eventually, we saved enough money, and we each made our purchases, something which, in today's money, would be equal to £1000.

In this instance, other than learning from other older childhood friends of our 'need' for this equipment, the only way to learn about the product and decide what to buy was to be on the shop floor in conversation with the sales representative.

Consider now how things are today and how differently we'd approach this purchase. Immediately upon thinking our need, most of us will pull out our phones and google. We'll quickly scroll through options and select something, learn about it and read the reviews. Once we're happy with the selection, we either buy it online, or we visit it in store.

Before now, I've walked out of the shop and declared to my friends "Great. I've brought cacao powder, hemp protein, bee pollen and that book we were just talking about", and they've looked at me baffled and said, "But they don't sell any of that in there?" "I know, but the line was ten people deep, what else was I gonna do waiting to pay for my sandwich", and waved the Amazon app on my phone at them.

For most of us, researching and buying online has become part of our everyday life. We buy online without seeing a product and trust the reviews of people we have never met. It's convenient, quick, and most importantly, led by us, the consumer.

Today, the majority of us only want to speak to a salesperson about our purchase if we can't find the information we need online or have specific requirements. Or want to talk our decision through with someone.

Either way, when we come to the conversation, we already have a pretty good idea of what we need, so our expectation of that salesperson is very different. If we have in-depth questions, we expect the person to help us and bring expertise and insights to the conversation that we couldn't access online. Simple answers and disinterest are the fastest way to turn a prospect off and send them straight into the arms of a competitor.

For many of our purchases, we can fulfil 100% of a buying decision online without speaking to anyone. If you feel shy or just hate the idea of sales, you might be tempted to design your business, so you don't have to speak to your prospects and have a sales conversation. For those of us who are experts in our field and not used to selling, this is a very natural response. However, when it comes to selling our core package, it won't work. We have to speak to our prospect.

Selling a Service

To make this easy for ourselves, we want to speak to our prospect when they are 57% of the way through their buying decision. Any sooner than this and we'll be wasting time and energy as, until the person has completed the earlier stages of the buying decision, they won't buy.

While we can replicate this with a structured sales conversation, it requires far more skill and has a high risk of taking up more time, and leading to multiple conversations and a lower conversion rate.

We can help our prospect reach 57% independently by creating content that supports them to research their problem, find out information and evaluate it and apply it to their situation.

When building our online content, marketing strategy, and sales funnel, we need to do it with the psychology of our prospect in mind. This means taking the time to consider the stages a person goes through to arrive at the point of investing in a solution and choosing the person they want to work with. For us, this is to identify the first 57% of their buying journey.

The final 43% is the sales conversation; our opportunity to get to know the prospect and determine if we can help them and if we want to.

"The final 43% is the sales conversation; our opportunity to get to know the prospect and determine if we can help them and if we want to."

Deciding whether we want to work with someone might seem like a strange way to look at things, especially if your business is new or you're desperate for clients, but in a service-based business, deciding whether to take on a client or not is probably one of the most important decisions you'll make. After all, you'll have to work with the client and deliver the service. There is nothing worse than having to come to work each day and to deal with demanding clients you don't like, knowing you are dependent on them for your survival.

Your happiness depends on having the right clients, and this is why the sales call is just as much for you to find out about the prospect as it is for the prospect to find out about you.

If you are like many experts who don't like the idea of doing 'sales', then I would ask you 'Will you be afraid to speak to your clients once you're working together?' I would suggest the answer is no, or at least unlikely, and this is the beauty of being a Trusted Advisor.

Most experts are not afraid to consult with their client to find out what their problems are and then provide solutions. They thrive on it. After all, it's the reason they chose to make a full-time career out of it and build a business doing what they love. Therefore, if you have no problem with this, you should have no problem with a sales call. It just comes down to how you approach the concept of 'sales', and how you interpret what you are doing.

"If you come in service with the view that you are here to help the person move forward, you will naturally demonstrate how good you are and how much the prospect needs to buy your services."

Recently, a client was expressing reservation about having sales calls, and as an IT professional, this wasn't surprising. Talking to people wasn't exactly his favourite thing to do. I helped him reframe this by casually asking "By the way, I know a company who are having trouble with their computer servers and want to know if they are set up efficiently; would you be able to speak to them and see if you can help?" My client readily agreed. I then confessed I was making it up, but did he see how easy the conversation appeared to him when it was a simple consultation to see if he can help?

Consulting on a problem, the problem you are expertly trained in is easy. The idea of sales is not. And yet, they are exactly the same thing.

It's just in how we are approaching the conversation and what we think we are doing. If we come in service with the view that we are there to help the person move forward, we will naturally demonstrate how good we are and how much the prospect needs to buy our services.

The thing we're going to do differently here is structure the call so we gather the information we need so both ourselves and the prospect can decide if we want to work together.

The key is to set up the sales appointment in just the right way, so we feel confident having the conversation and are in our natural flow. We need the prospect to come to us because they view us as an expert and someone they trust, someone whose advice they are grateful to receive. Cultivating this relationship begins by positioning our self as our prospect's Trusted Advisor by creating content that respects the natural buying journey of our prospect.

As our business is also time-sensitive, we need to build the business to accommodate how long it might take to win a deal. Depending on your business, it might take anywhere between 30 minutes to 9 months to confirm a deal. By understanding the buying journey of our prospects, we can create resources to shorten this time and aid the decision-making process dramatically. Hence, we invest in each prospect appropriately without it taking up too much time.

We do this by creating great content that matches how people buy.

The diagram on the double-page spread outlines the process prospects go through when making a buying decision.

Identify the Need

Before we can begin working with our prospects, they first have to recognise that they need what we offer. We want to be careful to not just classify someone as a prospect because they themselves have identified they have a problem and are interested in our service.

Very often, a person may have the problem we solve and a desperate need to solve it, but they will consider their situation normal and 'the way things are'. When we meet this person, we will know the issue immediately and can classify them as a prospect, even if the person isn't yet ready to recognise their situation.

This may seem strange, but the truth is most people are living with the status quo, believing that how things are is how things are. They don't recognise that things could be different. Instead, they continue to fight fires within their business and lives without recognising that they need not have the fire in the first place.

Take, for example, the recruitment industry. Within the industry, it is well known that the average turnover of staff is 60% per annum. Most companies have accepted this and budgeted accordingly. They've seen it as usual and not a problem—until now.

NEW LEAD

IDENTIFY

Create
Awareness

COMPLETE

Evidence

DIAGNOSE

Research

Self-
implement

INVEST

Transformational Package

Profile

SALES
APPOINTMENT

Sales
Conversation

SALE

© TheProfile.Company. All Rights Reserved.

In recent years, one enterprising individual, James Johnson of Nicoll Curtin, challenged this within his company and brought this figure down to 15% in his business, bucking all industry trends. Competing firms, who once took 60% as an industry norm that couldn't be changed, are now sitting up and realising that they could be doing things differently.

Just like the 4-minute mile that was once considered impossible, once it has been achieved, a new record is set, and 'excellence' has a new standard that must be reached.

The first step at cultivating new clients is to bring them to an awareness that they have a problem by helping them to identify they have a need.

Research

Once a person has become aware that they may have a problem and things may need to change, they will start to research the issue to determine if they do, in fact, have a problem and also what they should be doing about it. At this point, you won't know your prospect is thinking about you. They will read your online content but won't sign up for any offers. This is the next stage.

In our recruitment industry example, competitors who become aware of James Johnson's results will begin to question how he did it and whether they could achieve it themselves.

James isn't in the business of helping other recruitment first replicate his results, though. Thus, the industry will have to figure it out for themselves. They will have to do this by reading between the lines, consulting with experts and figuring out what he did that was so different.

In the world of Human Resources, this could be any manner of strategies and carefully managed variables. James' success leaves clues, but it doesn't leave a roadmap. Therefore, competitors will research an extensive number of methods and ideas, and read about a variety of subjects. They will evaluate their performance in each different area and whether they need to address this particular aspect within their business.

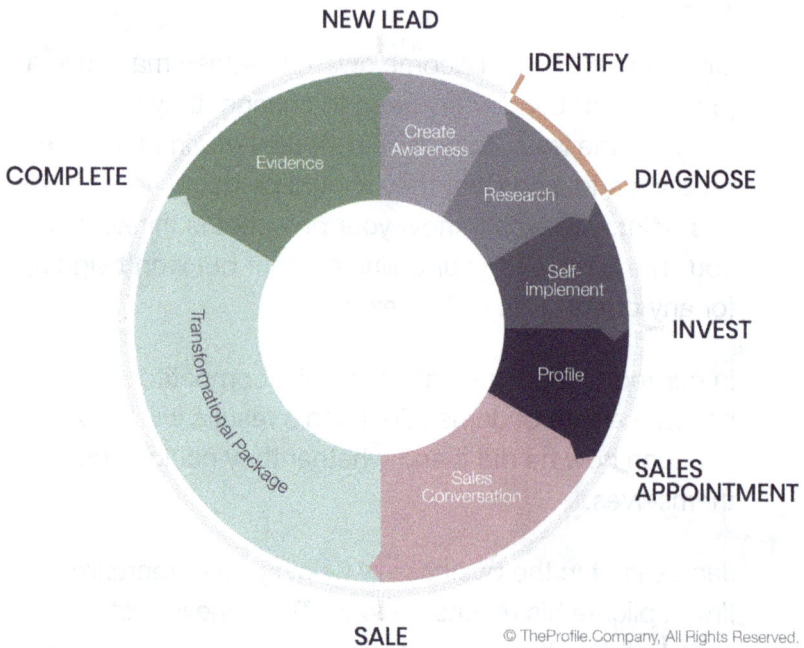

NEW LEAD

IDENTIFY

Create Awareness

Research

COMPLETE

Evidence

DIAGNOSE

Self-implement

Transformational Package

INVEST

Profile

Sales Conversation

SALES APPOINTMENT

SALE

© TheProfile.Company, All Rights Reserved.

In many respects, they are in the wilderness. They've come to recognise they have a problem, but they don't know a solution exists. Or if they do, they don't understand their problem to be able to hire in the right solution.

Enter the Trusted Advisor.

At this stage in the process, the prospect is researching how to replicate the same result as James, i.e. reduce employee turnover. They aren't researching employee compensation, ergonomic solutions or hiring processes because they haven't yet identified that that is why they can't keep their staff.

"In many respects, they are in the wilderness. They've come to recognise they have a problem, but they don't know a solution exists."

Before they can become interested in a solution, they first need to become aware of what their problem is. At this stage, we need to be supplying information that supports them in their research and helps them diagnose the problem. We want to be introducing potential issues and ways to evaluate their situation, but we don't want to get into how to solve the problem. This content will get ignored because until they feel confident about the problem they need to solve; they won't be interested in a solution.

Content that talks about the specifics of the hiring process or ergonomics is going to fall flat. It won't grab the person's interest at this stage because they don't know yet that ergonomics is the problem; all they know is their staff are leaving.

Instead, we want to create content that speaks about the symptoms of their problem and the consequence of living with it because it is this that will get their attention. Use words that get the person to say, 'that's me' (awareness) and then supply information that helps them to learn about the problem and evaluate their own performance. We want the person to diagnose they have this problem and seek to do something about it.

"Your content wants to speak about the symptoms of their problem and the consequence of living with it because it is this that will get their attention."

Interestingly, a few months after meeting with James and hearing about his results, I took on a new client who has a brand-new tool that transforms how recruitment companies hire their staff. By using it, recruitment agencies are promised a higher success of recruiting the right people for the business and thus reducing employee turnover.

When I first met them, their main focus was on creating content that explained the product and why recruitment was so important; content designed for people who had already recognised that the root of their problems lie in how they recruit.

What they didn't have was content focused on the big picture that would awaken their prospect to the fact they had a problem or that a result like 15% turnover is possible, so I put them in touch with James. Although they weren't responsible for James' results, by interviewing him and creating content around his story, they have the perfect opportunity to create awareness of what is possible and then pinpoint and signpost how to replicate his results.

The issue the prospect faces may not be recruitment, but by sharing this information, and inviting the prospect for a diagnostic, they will soon find out. By analysing James' results and creating a discussion around what James might be doing to achieve low employee turnover, the company are being of service to their marketplace. They are capturing their target market's attention and bringing them to an awareness of this new industry result and then adding value by openly discussing the likely reasons for his results.

This is helpful and informative content that will help their prospects begin to diagnose their own problem; and if it turns out that the reason the listeners staff are leaving is because they recruitment the wrong people, they will now have created and begun a relationship with their ideal prospect.

By keeping their content wide at this stage, they are getting their brand known by the target audience and positioning themselves as Trusted Advisors. They aren't forcing their solution on people and claiming that everyone's issue is the same; they are providing an arena to start a conversation and explore the issues. They aren't just appealing to people who know they need to improve their recruitment process; they are appealing to people who recognise they need to retain their staff which is a bigger pool of prospects providing a higher chance of finding new clients.

When creating our content, we need to start by thinking about the big picture. Does our prospect even recognise that they have a problem and, therefore, do they realise that it needs fixing?

When creating our content, we need to start by thinking about the big picture. Does our prospect even recognise that they have a problem within their business and, therefore, do they realise that it needs fixing? An out of the blue phone call talking about HR solutions is not going to reap results if the company don't recognise they need an external HR provider on hand to advise them.

In our recruitment industry example, competitors who become aware of James Johnson's results will begin to question how he did it and whether they could achieve it themselves.

One of my clients, Dianne Lambdin, provides outsourced HR solutions and specialises in creating the right company culture, i.e. great places to work. When writing her profile, it was essential to avoid talking about employment contracts and handbooks even though this is what she provides.

The types of companies she wants to attract are not 'turned on' by legal documents and such like. They are busy. They are growing their business. They are ambitious.

So, instead of talking about functional services, we need to talk about desirable results; things that our prospects desire to create but don't know how, or as yet, don't know that they don't know.

Working with the psychology of how people operate on LinkedIn, Dianne's opening paragraphs of the About Section read as follows:

Great places to work don't happen naturally. It doesn't matter how tech-savvy your company is, how in-demand you are, or how 'cool' your brand looks - if the culture isn't right, people won't want to work for you.

Companies like Google, Jaguar Land Rover, and John Lewis know this. Their company cultures weren't afterthoughts; they were central to their growth plans from the outset.

[NB These are just the first two paragraphs of her About section]

If you're a tech company looking to create a great place to work, this profile instantly tells you that there is more to it than flying by the seat of your pants. When companies are growing, they are in high demand and their brand is probably regarded as 'cool', but this shouldn't mean that the company can rest on their laurels and assume everything will work out naturally.

This opening paragraph quickly sets the context. It quickly lets us know what we are here to talk about and who we are talking to. It awakens a prospect to the fact they may have a problem. Plus, it will also awaken those who surround the prospect, that their friend, colleague or family member's ambitions may be thwarted if these issues aren't addressed, leading them to recommend you to them.

The LinkedIn Profile then goes on to demonstrate this by naming companies that are considered great to work at and pointing out that the company culture wasn't an afterthought. By doing this, we are awakening our target market to the need to look for a solution.

A great way to look at your marketing is to consider how you bought your last car. In the early stages of your buying journey, you'll want to research the market and see what is available. Specifics and detail are going to be the least of your concerns unless, of course, this stuff interests you.

Therefore, it is likely that if a salesperson opens the bonnet of the car you've just enquired about and starts talking specifics about the engine, you're going to be turned off. It's too early in the buying decision for this type of detail. Once you've narrowed your options down and have a clearer idea of what you might like to buy, this information will become relevant.

Details are only relevant when a prospect is in the final stage of a buying decision. The point at which they know they are likely to invest and need more information to make the right choice.

When a prospect is just beginning to identify they have a need, we want to create content that talks about desired results, transformations and things that will make our prospects stop in their tracks and take notice. In the Research Stage, we need to help our prospect diagnose their problem and understand it.

"Details are only relevant when a prospect is in the final stage of a buying decision. The point at which they know they are likely to invest and need more information to make the right choice."

In Dianne's profile, we quickly identify the need *"great places to work don't happen naturally",* and we begin the research stage by pinpointing that *"If the company culture isn't right, people won't work for you"*. Now, our prospect knows that they need to have a conversation about culture. What they don't know at this stage is that an important part of creating a company culture is by having the right employee contracts, employee handbooks, and compensation plans in place. Right now, they aren't interested. They simply want to know whether their company culture is helping or hindering their ability to attract and retain staff and if they should do something about it.

The Psychology of How People Buy

The following diagram outlines the stages a person goes through to make a buying decision.

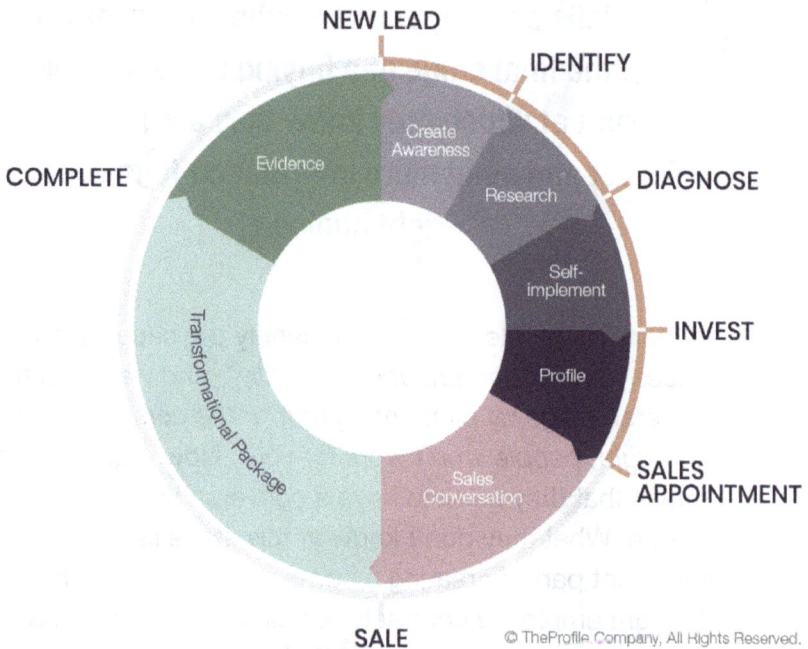

NEW LEAD

IDENTIFY

DIAGNOSE

COMPLETE

Create Awareness

Evidence

Research

Self-implement

INVEST

Transformational Package

Profile

SALES APPOINTMENT

Sales Conversation

SALE

© TheProfile Company, All Rights Reserved.

NEW LEAD: Social Media has made it possible to appeal to a prospect who doesn't yet know they have a problem that needs solving. Previously, our marketing would only reach prospects that had already identified they had a problem and were in the process of researching solutions using keywords. Now, however, we can pitch our message to a wide variety of people who aren't actively looking for solutions and awaken them to the fact that actually what they are experiencing is really a symptom of a problem that could easily be solved.

IDENTIFY: Once the person has identified they may have a problem, they will begin researching it in order to define what the problem is and fully diagnose it.

DIAGNOSE: Once the person is sure they have the problem and are clear on what it is and the impact it is having on them, they will begin to research solution and implement them independently. It is only when they realise that they can't do this entirely alone, that the problem is bigger than them and requires more than the free advice available online, that they will consider investing in a solution.

INVEST: Once a person has decided to invest in a solution, it will come down to who they trust to help them. This could be someone they know well or someone they have built trust with online digesting their content. If you have covered each part of the buying journey successfully, that person will be you.

SALES APPOINTMENT: Now they have decided that they want to invest in a solution and that you could be the right person, they will need to speak to you. In a time-sensitive business, this conversation needs to have direction and a clear structure. It needs to walk the prospect back over the buying journey, so they are reassured they have made the right conclusions, and for you, that this is someone who really needs your help.

Diagnose

Now that the prospect has awoken to the fact that they have a problem and have begun researching solutions, we need to assist our prospect in diagnosing whether they have a problem and the extent to which they have it.

In the example with James at Nicoll Curtin, there really are few resources available to help companies replicate his results because he isn't in the business of teaching others to do the same. Thus, we are left with just the hints as to what he did differently and but no definitive answers pointing to an exact solution.

> **"It is important to access the situation with them and not assume that they have correctly identified the root cause of their problem and that your solutions are what they need."**

If the difference James made was company culture, then Dianne's profile would resonate with James' competitors. Having identified that 60% annual staff turnover doesn't have to be an industry norm, these companies will begin researching how to change their culture, but just because they think the culture is their issue, doesn't necessarily mean that it is. Remember the client isn't an expert, and it is highly unlikely that they will be able to diagnose their issue correctly.

Their issue might be company culture, or it might be the hiring process. Another of my clients would argue that low employee retention rates are due to CEOs having poor leadership skills, and this is the first place any company looking to retain their staff should look.

There are many different opinions, many different diagnoses that can be given for exactly the same situation. The only people that can honestly know what the issue is and advise on the solution is the qualified professional with years of experience, i.e. the expert.

As a Trusted Advisor, it is at this stage that we need to step in and help. A client should not be left to purchase a solution based on their own assessment. Instead, part of our service is to help prospects diagnose their problem and point them to other professionals if our service isn't the right solution for them.

If a company has reached out to you, it is important to access the situation with them and not assume that they have correctly identified the root cause of their problem and that your solutions are what they need. Instead, we need to take the time to diagnose the problem and say if we don't think our solution is the right approach for them.

When a person is indecisive, it simply means they haven't completed the necessary parts of the buying journey.

This level of engagement will leave our prospect confident that they have diagnosed their situation correctly and that they have found an expert capable of helping them. By adding value like this, you are demonstrating your abilities and building a relationship. The level of trust this creates will increase the likelihood of you winning their business.

When we do this well, we not only increase the chance of the person saying yes to us, but we also speed up the likelihood of them saying yes. We can avoid months of unnecessary follow-up and indecision. When a person is indecisive, it simply means they haven't completed the necessary parts of the buying journey and are unsure.

If they say "I need to think about it", it means that a part of the buying journey was not completed, something that can be avoided with the right content and the right line of questioning during a sales call.

Self-Implementation

Once the prospect has identified what their problem is, they will need a plan of action for solving it. If you haven't yet spoken to the prospect or haven't made a strong enough case for investing in a solution, they will begin to implement solutions on their own.

With so much information freely available, this isn't hard. People will want to give something their best go before hiring In an expert. If they can learn it from a book or follow the steps in a video and solve their own problem, they will do so. This is why we need to be ready with the right content. Content that tells a prospect how to solve their problem independent of us.

If a person can solve their problem using free or low-priced resources, this means they didn't have a big enough problem to qualify as our ideal prospect. Remember, we only want to work on projects that excite us, sharpen our skills, and create transformational results, the type that people talk about.

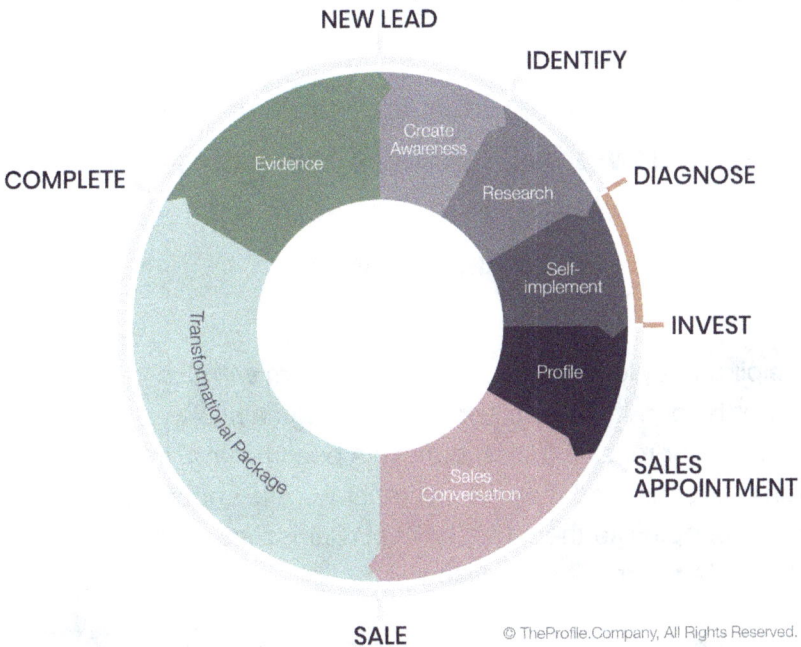

NEW LEAD

IDENTIFY

COMPLETE

DIAGNOSE

Create Awareness

Evidence

Research

Self-implement

INVEST

Transformational Package

Profile

SALES APPOINTMENT

Sales Conversation

SALE

© TheProfile.Company, All Rights Reserved.

We don't want clients with small problems because, unless the solution 'wow's them, they will likely resent investing in our solution, a dynamic that could lead to a tense relationship and lower our reputation. After all, our reputation is made up of what people say about us, and we want everyone who talks about us to do so with enthusiasm and excitement.

Thus, we want less than ideal prospects, those with small problems, to use our free content and disqualify themselves from our sales process. We only want people who recognise they have a big problem that free content can't easily solve, to progress through our sales funnel. We only want clients who recognise they need to invest a solution if they are going to get the results they desperately need.

> **"If a person can solve their problem using free or low-priced resources, this means they didn't have a big enough problem to qualify as our ideal prospect."**

Helping people to solve their own problem will also work in our favour. If we help someone through a sticky situation or resolve an issue they've been having, they will remember us, and they will tell other people about us - other people like them that have similar issues. It really is the perfect form of advertising.

Although they weren't our ideal prospect, they are in community with our target market and will come into contact with people who also need our solution and could well be an ideal client for us. As they have first-hand experience of the results we help people create, it will be natural for them to mention our name and give a powerful recommendation in our favour.

As more people digest our content, the higher the chance the right prospect - the one who can't solve their problem using free content - will filter through and raise their hand to want to work with us.

Since they will have digested our content by the time they speak to us, we can be sure they have already begun to diagnose their problem and identify they need to invest in a solution, and with us.

In our time-sensitive businesses, this is exactly what we want.

Within the free content we create, we want to provide practical steps and 'how-to' information, with our personal philosophy and our methodology embedded. This way, our prospect is not only getting the answers they are looking for but are also gaining further insight into the extent of the problem. The more we help them, the more they will understand their problem and the closer they will be to deciding they need to invest in a solution.

"The more we help, the more they will understand their problem and the closer they will be to deciding they need to invest in a solution."

The more exposure they have to us, the more confident they will be in choosing us as their service provider, and ultimately, the better the working relationship.

When I wrote my book What to Put on Your LinkedIn Profile, I wrote it in service to my marketplace, recognising that I could never write profiles for all 660 million LinkedIn members. I also knew that many people would read the introduction outlining the importance of a profile, look at the remaining pages and conclude the profile was too important for them to attempt to do it on their own and would opt to hire me instead.

I also knew that a large proportion wouldn't be in a position to hire me and therefore would use the resource to give it their best go and be grateful to me for the helping hand. I also recognised that people talk, and the best tool I could provide to make sure I was part of their conversation was an introduction to my philosophy and methodology. Not everyone will agree with it, but it will still be part of the conversation. I also knew that someone could read the entire book and still want to work with me. Thus, giving away all the practical steps and methodology made perfect sense.

By writing a book, I positioned myself as an expert. I also allowed people to get to know me and my approach, and then choose me. I made it easy for people to respect their own budgets and say 'no' when they didn't want to buy and to say 'yes' when they really could perceive, for themselves, the return on investment they would achieve if they had me do it for them instead, i.e. my ideal prospect.

When we just skip over these steps and jump to selling our product, we put ourselves up against our competition. We end up fighting for a very small segment of the marketplace, i.e. those who have already identified they have a problem and are ready to invest.

Approaching people who are actively looking for your solution might sound like a good idea and less effort than convincing someone who doesn't know they have a problem, but it's when we go after a prospect who is already actively looking to buy that we place ourselves against our competition — a much smaller marketplace.

"When we go after a prospect who is already actively looking to buy, we place ourselves against our competition — a much smaller marketplace."

Prospects who already know they have a problem and are actively researching solutions tend to talk to multiple providers and buy on price. They have options and can negotiate. However, when we begin the conversation with a prospect and bring them to an awareness of the problem, the strength of our relationship with them is such that they wouldn't look anywhere else or consider buying from another provider to save a bit of cash because they trust us and our approach.

Prospects at the Self-Implementation stage will already have a clear idea of the problem they need to solve and the keywords to start their searches with. This is where SEO (Search Engine Optimisation) comes into play.

If your prospect has already recognised they have a problem and is looking for a solution, they will begin to search online using keywords. This is when you want your training content to appear. Your prospect thinks they have some idea of the problem and is looking for quick solutions and more information.

In my business, the majority of people will come to appreciate the value of a LinkedIn profile by talking to others in their business community. However, they won't necessarily have realised that their profile should be written differently to a CV. So, while I have a captive market of people looking for short tutorials on how to do technical things, I can't assume that people googling for answers already know about the different approach or that they are ready to invest in a solution.

Thus, I provide the content they are searching for. By doing so, I create an opportunity to start a dialogue and educate them. The technical answers I provide are always short and waffle free, but within the instructions, I embed hints that there may be 'more to this'. It is those who have a need that will pick up on these hints and want to find out more.

At this point, I begin a relationship with the prospect, and after they've digested what they need to answer their immediate question, they will either opt to learn more or approach me for one-on-one help. What I want is for the prospect to already "know, like and trust" me by the time they make contact and, better yet, they know they have a problem they want to invest in.

Using YouTube, Facebook, LinkedIn and other trusted platforms, we can begin answering the questions our prospects are asking and position ourselves as their trusted expert. The content we provide needs to be in a variety of formats, such as reading, watching and listening, so our prospects can select the learning mode that best suits them.

The more content we provide, the more we demonstrate our expertise and position ourselves as our prospects' Trusted Advisor. It is at this point we fulfil our prospects' need to spend those critical 7-hours before the Zero Moment of Truth when they decide to buy from us.

Invest

If we've followed the above stages correctly, we'll have moved our prospect from not knowing they have a problem and therefore not looking for a solution, to knowing they have a problem. If we've created the right content during the Self-Implementation stage, an ideal prospect will have concluded that they can't solve the problem using free content and they need to invest in a solution.

At the point the prospect has decided they need to invest in a solution, we want to invite them to a sales appointment. Before they will do this, though, they first need to know they trust us and could see themselves working with us. I

f we have been responsible for bringing the prospect to the conclusion that they need help, they should already have a strong relationship with us. They should already know our credentials and trust us as their expert.

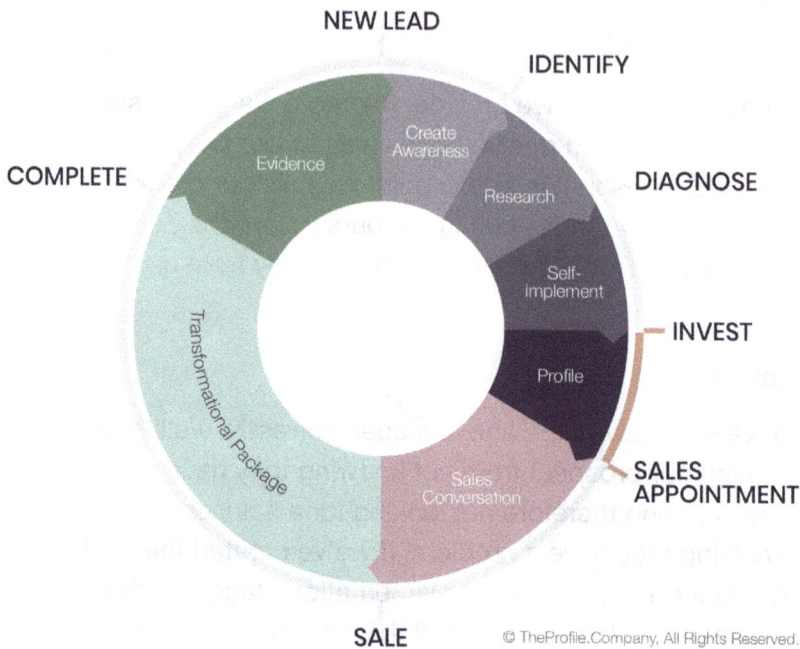

NEW LEAD

IDENTIFY

Create Awareness

Evidence

Research

COMPLETE

DIAGNOSE

Self-implement

INVEST

Transformational Package

Profile

SALES APPOINTMENT

Sales Conversation

SALE

© TheProfile.Company, All Rights Reserved.

If the person is still unsure of us, or they have come to us via a different path, our online profile will become critical at this point.

When someone is ready to invest, they will want to know how we can help them. Before a person is willing to reach out, they need to have some idea of what working with us will look like and if they trust us to be able to deliver the solution.

Even if someone has had their Zero Moment of Truth with us (the 7 hours, 11 touchpoints in 4 locations), they will still do a final assessment to determine if they trust us before reaching out.

Building Trust Through Content

Last year, I received an email via my shopping cart to say I had recently received a payment of £75. Curious, I opened the email to see that someone in the USA had purchased a LinkedIn Profile Review from me, something I provided for free at the time but had listed on my shopping cart as a paid item.

Making sure my automated system was working properly, I checked my online calendar, and sure enough, the same person has scheduled time to speak with me using the link provided in the response email.

When we had the profile session, it was clear the person was already familiar with my content and my approach. Before we were halfway through the session, she asked: "How can you help me?" Blown away with the free advice I was providing over the phone, and what she had read online, she already knew she wanted to work with me. Within twenty minutes of talking, she had bought my core package, spending nearly £3000.

When I asked her how she came across me, she said "I recognised that my LinkedIn profile was an important tool going forward and was updating it myself. I couldn't do something, so I googled it, and your blog post came up. It helped me fix the issue, but what you said, along with the instructions, really got my attention so I dug around some more, read lots of your content, watched one of your webinars and then I saw I could book an appointment to talk to you. I knew I had to, so I did". This is a perfect example of how creating the right content wins you business.

Our LinkedIn Profile, website, blogs, online reviews etc., all come into play at this point. If all you have is a LinkedIn Profile, that is fine. What's important is that you look good where you can be found.

"If we fail to provide the right information about ourselves at this stage, we leave our prospects unsure about us and our service, and thus could well lead our prospect to fall into the arms of our competitors."

How long a person spends at each stage depends on how much time people have spent with your content, how you present yourself, and how ready they feel to trust you. Once they have completed the stages of their own buying journey, though, they should be ready to reach out to book a sales appointment with you.

If we fail to provide the right information about ourselves at this stage, we leave our prospects unsure about us and our service, and thus could well lead our prospect to fall into the arms of our competitors. We may have done a good job cultivating the lead, helping the person identify they have a problem and helping them diagnose it correctly while recognising they need more than an online tutorial to fix it. Still, if we fail to look credible, they will take this information and try to find someone else who they do think is credible to help them instead.

It's important to note here that looking credible is about how you show up more than it is about where and how often you show up. In the early stages of developing your business, you may not have a website or much content, but that shouldn't stop you going at your business with all you've got.

LinkedIn is the perfect tool for this as the profile is comprehensive and allows you to share the types of information your prospect will be looking for. For more information on how to put your LinkedIn Profile together, go to www.TheProfile.Company.

"If we fail to provide the right information about ourselves at this stage, we leave our prospects unsure about us and our service, and thus could well lead our prospect to fall into the arms of our competitors."

During the Profile stage of the buying journey, we also want to tell our prospects how we work with our clients. We want our prospect to come to a sales appointment with us fully equipped with the information they need to decide if they're going to work with us, and this includes time evaluating our packages.

Therefore, it's important that we share our packages and outline our product eco-system. We can do this in the Experience entry of our LinkedIn profile for our current business. By outlining how we help people, we allow our prospect to 'see' themselves doing it and consider whether our approach will work for them. This way, when they come to the call, they have already considered it thoroughly and are "pre-sold". They know they want to work with us for who we are, and they know our method will work for them.

Booking the Sales Appointment

The first thing we need to note here is that no one likes attending sales appointments. The idea of having a conversation where you may have to say 'no' to someone is uncomfortable for the majority of people. The offer of a 'sales appointment' makes people feel nervous and creates a feeling of social awkwardness and unwanted pressure.

What if they don't want to buy in the end? What if they have to say no to you? What if the person they are speaking to manipulates them into buying something really expensive that they later come to regret?

Therefore, as we said earlier, we have to present the sales appointment differently and mean it. In my office, I use the term 'sales appointment' to let my colleagues know the type of conversation I am having and how to respect my space during an important phone call.

However, in all other conversations, I am providing a LinkedIn Profile Review. This isn't manipulative. I really am providing a review of their profile with the full intention of adding value. It's just that, at the beginning of the call, I've asked permission to pitch my solution to them if we both agree it could be a good fit. This gives me permission to ask for their business at the end of the call if I think it is the right solution for them, while allowing us to be present to the content of the call, without feeling the pressure to buy. So, how do we get the person to attend a sales appointment, be it face-to-face or over the phone?

"The key is to provide an enticing hook, so the person wants to speak to you and feels safe doing so."

The key is to provide an enticing hook, so the person wants to speak to you and feels safe doing so. This means providing value. For one of my clients, selling coaching services, having a simple conversation or free session doesn't work. The type of person he is reaching out to isn't interested in talking about their feelings with another guy or asking for help. What they are interested in, though, is an assessment of 'How am I doing?'.

My client Dave's hook, therefore, is a 60-minute diagnostic that reveals to the company director how well they are performing in six critical areas. He didn't invent the six critical areas; he just built upon them and made his own diagnostic and content around leading industry research. The result is something that provides real insight into the extent of the problem and the need to invest in a solution to resolve it should it prove necessary.

His offer attracts his ideal audience and will have them reveal the information he needs to be able to determine if he can help them. It provides something of tangible value that is attractive to the prospect and will have them want to attend the appointment.

Diagnostics, scorecards, reviews and feedback are the perfect option as they give the person something tangible to work with that goes beyond simply outlining your services and hoping they say 'yes'. That's like going for the marriage proposal when you've just started talking on Tinder.

A well thought out Sales Conversation will also allow you to explore your prospects' problem in-depth and help diagnose it correctly. With the right approach, you'll be able to connect your prospect to the urgency of fixing the problem and not delaying.

Getting this hook right is imperative since it is only by having a sales appointment and talking to our prospects that we have any chance of winning new business, and therefore, having a business. As we said at the beginning of this book, our entire objective is to book a sales appointment.

"A good hook invites a conversation and an opportunity to explore the issues in a safe environment that helps our prospect move forward."

If people aren't taking up our offer, it means our hook is not compelling enough. Most of the people who take a LinkedIn Profile Review with me do so out of curiosity, not because they already know they want to invest in having someone do it for them. Dave has company directors request a review with him out of curiosity, not because they perceive they have a problem and want to hire a coach.

A good hook invites a conversation and an opportunity to explore the issues in a safe environment that helps a prospect move forward. You will want to include your hook on your LinkedIn profile and website and be ready to invite people to it whether in conversation, face-to-face, or during online interactions.

The most efficient and best way to do this is to use an online booking tool that integrates with your diary and at an advanced level, your CRM (customer relationship tool). When someone expresses an interest, all you need to do is send them the link, and they can schedule their appointment. This method saves the time of going back and forth, confirming appointments, and it makes it easier for the person to cancel and reschedule without it impacting or inconveniencing your day. It is one of the most important parts of creating a sustainable, time-sensitive business.

Personally, I used OnceHub, but there are others on the market, including Hubspot, Calendly and SimplyBook.

The Sales Conversation

Now you have the person on the phone or in a face-to-face meeting you need to deliver value. You also need to respect that your prospect may not have visited each step in the buying journey and are only with you out of curiosity to hear how your diagnostic rates them.

You also need to appreciate that, if they have gone through the buying process thus far, they may have misdiagnosed themselves.

Part of the role of a Trusted Advisor is to be honest with them and if they don't need your service, tell them so.

A sales appointment can't be a simple chat. It needs to be carefully structured to follow the natural buying process of a prospect. A carefully constructed script will ensure you are always in control of the conversation and able to lead your prospect to make the right decision for them and do it within the allotted time.

During the call, you need to share critical advice and information to help your prospect resolve their situation, even if that means they don't need to invest in your solution. So this means being honest. If your solution costs £1000 to buy, but you can see they would be better spending the £1000 elsewhere at this time, we need to tell them. This is what it means to be an advisor and a trusted one. It means advising correctly even if it means we miss out on what we desperately want, i.e. a new sale.

Since our business is time-sensitive, we need to be clear about the length of the appointment and stick to it. Good practice for this is organising your appointments back-to-

back with 15 minutes leeway in between. This will ensure you develop the discipline to complete calls within the allotted time. Spending several hours in sales mode will also help you develop and hone your skills, as you can implement new learning and distinctions on your next call and immediately see the results.

There is also a big difference in mindset from "doing" sales to doing admin or technical tasks, such that it can take a while to switch from one mode to another, so holding back-to-back sales appointments and gaining momentum is the best way to ensure your success.

In my business, I don't allow impromptu LinkedIn Profile Reviews. The times that I have provided a review without an appointment have usually resulted in long conversations and no sale, simply because neither party is in the right frame of mind and the foundations of the call, the structure, have not been laid down properly.

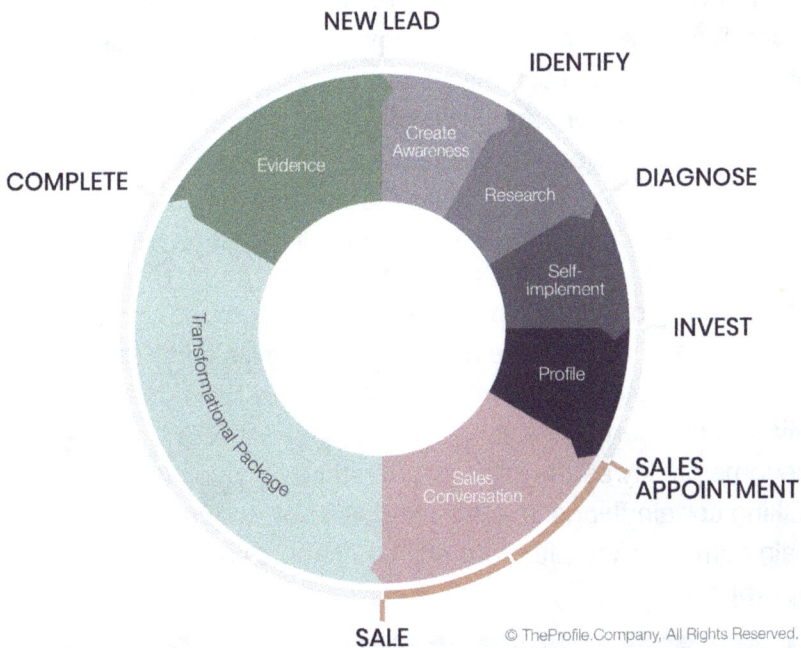

NEW LEAD

IDENTIFY

COMPLETE

DIAGNOSE

Create Awareness

Evidence

Research

Self-implement

INVEST

Profile

Transformational Package

SALES
APPOINTMENT

Sales Conversation

SALE

© TheProfile.Company, All Rights Reserved.

The sales script is one of the most important things you can have in your business. Simply put, they get the job done. With a clear opening and a clear end, you will ensure that you frame the session correctly and remain in control. A clear opening will tell the prospect what to expect during your time together and put people at ease. It will let them know you have a plan, and they just have to trust you to do what you do best.

> ## "Since our business is time-sensitive, we need to be clear about the length of the appointment and stick to it."

A script doesn't mean that you read it word for word like a robot, but rather that you know how to frame each stage of the sales call and say things concisely in a way the prospect can understand. It is, of course, something that, when perfected, you can hire a team to do and be confident that they will replicate the same results as you. It is an asset within the business that will help it grow.

The opening of your script needs to set the groundwork. At the start of the call, we need to ask permission to ask personal questions about the challenge they have. Missing this part of the script can mean prospects become prickly as they don't understand why you are asking certain things. It is also at this point we want to gain permission to pitch our solution should we deem it appropriate.

Do you have the assets in place you need to succeed in your business? Take the Scorecard and find out how much of what we're talking about , you already have in place. http://www.theprofile.company/scorecard

If the prospect is pre-sold, they should be invested enough to feel comfortable divulging sensitive and personal information about themselves and/or their business. If you've set the stage correctly, this should be no problem. If you find people questioning why you are asking certain questions or being cagey, you know there is more work to be done on your script to set the stage for the appointment. You will need to improve your opening script.

Having permission to present your services is critical and easy to obtain at the beginning of the call when you are offering to exchange value with them. All you are saying is 'My objective is to provide you with as much value as possible. If you feel you can take my advice and make it happen, that's great; if not, we can talk about how I help, but there is no obligation. If you don't think it's for you, we don't have to have that conversation'. This puts people at ease and opens up the conversation for the work that needs to be done to determine if you're a good fit for one another.

In a previous chapter, we mentioned LAPS. Leads, Appointments, Presentations, Sales. Right now, we are talking about the appointment. However, it is the Presentation at the end of the session, where the magic happens.

The Presentation

A presentation is simply where you outline how you can help. During the sales conversation, you will have ascertained whether the person has a real need and if you are the right person to help them. If you have discovered that they aren't the right type of client or you can see they wouldn't get a return on investment working with you, you can simply tell them this and part company. You may point them at additional resources that can help or refer them to someone more suitable.

After you've finished providing very clear advice and direction, a powerful question to ask is: 'Is that something you feel you can do yourself or do you think you might like my help?' When I ask this question, the majority of people gush that they don't think they could possibly do it themselves and instantly ask for the information. They either ask how I can help and purchase, or they immediately say 'Yes, of course, I need your help, but I don't think I can afford it'. This type of response allows us to know exactly where to go next with the conversation.

"A great presentation will outline how your services apply to their situation and how it will solve the unique challenges you've just been hearing about."

It is at this point we have permission to outline how we can help, and we achieve the P of LAPS. The presentation. Without a presentation, there is no chance of a sale.

A great presentation will outline how your services apply to their situation and how it will solve the unique challenges you've just been hearing about. You need to keep it tight and timely, avoiding waffle and nervous chatter. Once you've outlined how you can help and why it is a great solution for them, you need to mention your price. Then, ask the buying question. 'Is that something you'd like to go ahead with?' and then you wait for their answer.

In some instances, and in some businesses, this may mean submitting a proposal or getting other decision-makers involved. Ideally, though, you will have ascertained this at the beginning of the call or even before the appointment was booked.

If there are others involved, you need to factor this in and create content that will help your prospect to close the deal. The person you are speaking to may be completely sold on what you do and be a raving fan, but never rely on them to be able to pitch your services and sell you to their colleagues. Instead, develop some resources that you can forward that will aid them. This might be a video, a download, a recording of your chat together, and most certainly, a copy of your brochure. It is a good idea to consider who the decision-maker is and who surrounds them, as you'll need to create content for them.

It's important to understand that our prospects and our clients are all surrounded by people we can't see. People who care about them and want the best for them. People that, even though our prospect holds the authority to buy, question their decisions and have them question whether they made the right choice.

When people tell others about the solution they've bought from you, they are also telling others about their challenge. The person they are talking to may have something to say about the challenge or another perspective on how it could be fixed, including another service provider they trust that they'd rather them work with. It might be that the other person isn't the right person, that they haven't successfully diagnosed the problem, and this is where what you did during the sales call and how you show up online, really comes into play.

> **"The person you are speaking to may be completely sold on what you do and be a raving fan but never rely on them to be able to pitch your services and sell you to their colleagues."**

Our new client needs to be very sure about their decision and be able to justify to themselves and others, confidently, why this decision is right for them. This is achieved by making sure they fully understand what we are doing and why and having the right resources available.

If we fail to do this, we could end up with an unhappy client with buyer's remorse, who is difficult to work with.

The Follow Up

If you don't win the sales during the first call, you will need to have other resources to nurture your prospect and keep them warm. By continuing to think of them and send helpful resources that support them, you will stay front of mind, and remain positioned as their Trusted Advisor.

For big companies, following up via LinkedIn is critical as decisions take time. You'll need to factor this into your sales process and sales projections. People often move jobs, and often, multiple people are involved in the decision. If this is the case for your product or service, I recommend using LinkedIn's product Sales Navigator to track key people and nurture the lead with relevant content and conversation.

In some industries, following up won't feel so comfortable. Personally, I don't like to follow up just because if an individual thought it was right for them, they would have said yes at the time or come back to me.

Phoning up and asking off the cuff 'do you want to do this?' is a tricky conversation that makes both of sides feel uncomfortable, especially since the invitation to speak initially was pitched as a no-obligation call designed to add value. Following up aggressively and putting people on the spot by phoning when they least expect it violates this agreement. Plus, if the call was correctly structured, both parties should have left the conversation clear on whether the product was a good fit or not.

Other industry professionals may disagree with this, but before deciding which approach is right for you, I'd encourage you to check your social compass and ascertain whether following up feels right. If you feel nervous, this could be because following up with someone is nerve-racking and a step outside of your comfort zone, or it could be that it is the wrong action to take and your discomfort is a sign that you're violating your agreement with the prospect.

The best way to get around these issues is to ensure you're connected on LinkedIn. Along with posting relevant content to stay at the front of your prospect's mind, you can also send short, non-intrusive messages asking how your prospect is getting on, as well as forward resources you think might help them.

You can stay in touch and front of mind with an automated series of emails, status updates, blogs, graphics or you might keep a resource library of content you can attach to add value when sending follow up emails.

Exercise

Before moving on to the next chapter, why not take a moment to consider how you will apply the content.

What symptoms will a prospect, who needs your help, likely have? What words and phrases will they likely use when sharing with others?

What are the key questions and challenges a prospect googles when trying to solve this problem?

What content could you provide to support your prospect find answers? (Self-Implementation)

Why we should always take the time to explain our process before the sale

Several months back, I recognised I needed to invest in a solution, so I called the first person I knew who provided it. She took my project on and got to work. A few days later, I attended a networking event where a new person independently identified my need and began guiding me through how to do it myself. He too was an expert in this area and a provider I could have turned to.

His explanation really helped me to understand how to go about things and what to do. I was so excited by his knowledge and ideas that I wanted to work with him. Only I was already committed elsewhere. I told him this and he gave me a few pointers to speak to my provider about.

The response I got from my provider was a brush off. It was awkward because I didn't want to appear to be telling her how to do her job or that she was wrong. However, the lack of insight into her process made me nervous and left me questioning her methods.

We didn't get any results from the campaign, nor did she conduct a debrief at the end to explain what she did and why we spent £600 on ads to achieve no new sales. From what I can tell, she didn't use any of the advanced methods the guy at the networking event talked me through and, to this day, I am convinced I didn't get the best service or that she is an expert in her field, and this is sad.

This is why we want to avoid simply saying 'Yes I can help' and jumping into the project. Instead, we want to take the time before the sale is agreed to talk about what is needed, why it is needed and our method. No matter how convinced someone is at the beginning of the conversation that they want to work with us, we still need to do due diligence and establish the right footing for the working relationship.

This step should never be overlooked. It's important that we do it correctly because every project we undertake reinforces our expertise and either provides evidence we can achieve results for our clients or leaves us and our marketing place wondering. Every client we take on is someone who may recommend us to someone else, or who might be called upon to give us a reference. "Fred, you worked with John, how was it?" We don't want to leave them floundering because they were disappointed with our work. When someone expresses interest to work with us, we need to revert back to the beginning of the buying cycle.

Key Takeaways

- When we understand how people buy, we can invest our time making the type of content and information that best suits our marketplace.

- People don't call businesses to ask simple questions, they google. If we don't provide this information they will return to their search and find someone who does, i.e. your competitor.

- A sales conversation is really a chance to learn about a person's problem and ascertain if we can help. When we approach it this way, the nerves around 'sales' disappears.

- Our prospect won't necessarily have diagnosed their problem correctly, and part of our job is to help them – even if it means sending the prospect to another provider.

- We want to avoid talking about the functional parts of the service we offer, but, instead, the outcomes it will create.

- People don't attend 'sales' appointments, but they are interested in exploring their issues in a safe environment designed to help them move forward.

Seeing it in motion

8. Seeing it in Motion

The stages of the buying journey can easily be depicted in this diagram. The circular diagram shows how your relationship with a prospect develops as they progress through their buying decision. We can use this diagram to create appropriate content to match each stage of their journey.

The buying journey can take anything between five minutes to nine months, depending on your prospect. A prospect might need to digest all the content before they opt into a diagnostic sales appointment, or they may simply say yes because they have spoken to you at an event or read your LinkedIn profile and it just feels right to them.

Stages of the Buying Journey

NEW LEAD: Social Media has made it possible to appeal to a prospect who doesn't yet know they have a problem that needs solving. Previously, our marketing would only reach prospects that had already identified they had a problem and were in the process of researching solutions using keywords. Now, however, we can pitch our message to a wide variety of people who aren't actively looking for solutions and awaken them to the fact that what they are experiencing is a symptom of a problem that could easily be solved.

CREATE AWARENESS

The Prospect who doesn't know they have a problem isn't looking for a solution.

They are utterly unaware that life is harder than it needs to be and consider themselves normal.

IDENTIFY: Your content resonates with your prospect, and they say, "This is me".

RESEARCH: Once the person has identified they may have a problem, they will begin researching it to understand it further and fully diagnose their situation.

The Prospect knows they have a problem but don't know a solution already exists.

They know something isn't right and may, or may not, know what. They aren't actively looking for a solution because they believe that this is just how life is, and no solution exists.

SELF-IMPLEMENTATION

Prospects know they have a problem and are looking for a solution.

They have successfully diagnosed their problem and know all the keywords to accurately Google solutions, and begin utilising free content and advice online.

DIAGNOSE: Once the person is sure they have the problem and the impact it is having on them; they will begin to research solutions and implement them independently. It is only when they realise that they can't do this entirely alone, that the problem is bigger than them and requires more than the free advice available online, that they will consider investing in a solution.

INVEST: Once a person has decided to invest in a solution, they will begin looking for a service provider to help them. If they have spent plenty of time with your content, and/or completed their buying journey with you, there should be no question that it is you that they call. If they don't call you, and you realise they are going to work with your competitors, then you know that your profile, as in whether you show up online as a credible source, is the issue.

PROFILE: They recognise that free or low-price content is not going to provide them with the results they desperately need, and they will need to invest in professional support. They begin researching who to hire, looking closely at the credentials and believability of available providers.

SALES APPOINTMENT: Now that they have decided they want to invest in a solution and that you could be the right person, they will need to speak to you. In a time-sensitive business, this conversation needs to have direction and a clear structure. It needs to walk the prospect back over the buying journey, so they are reassured they have made the right conclusions, and for you, that this is someone who needs your help.

The individual books a sales diagnostic with you attracted by your offer to provide insights into their situation with no obligation to buy. When speaking to individuals authorised to make purchases independently (because it is their own business or they are authorised to spend up to a value), the 30-minute diagnostic call should be adequate. However, a decision requires multiple decision-makers; further stages will be required before a sale can be confirmed. These stages occur within this section.

SALE: Having shared their situation with you and heard your advice, the prospect decides that they want to work with you. You process the sale and set up the first stages of your transformational package.

The deal is agreed, and paperwork is finalised. You set the first appointment and prepare to start work.

TRANSFORMATIONAL PACKAGE: You lead someone through the stages of your package, making sure they hit each milestone and achieve the outcome you promised.

You deliver your full service, taking your prospect through each milestone until you have achieved the outcome agreed to.

COMPLETE: You both agree that what you set out to do was achieved and the agreement has been fulfilled. Both parties are now free of their obligations.

EVIDENCE: Looking at the results you achieved together and what your solution is now allowing your client to do, you create testimonials, case-studies, status updates, and add to your portfolio. When writing, aim to add plenty of insights that create awareness, so anyone reading it from your target market will say "this is me" and begin their buying journey.

The Modern Buying Cycle

As we mentioned before, the advent of the internet has changed how people purchase. Looking at the traditional buying journey, you'll notice it starts with 'Identify a Need', however, in the modern buying journey, you will notice that this is actually the second point that identified on the clock as 1 o'clock. This is because, with social media, we have the ability to find brand new prospects who haven't yet identified they have a need and bring them to an awareness of their problem. Something that previously was very hard to do.

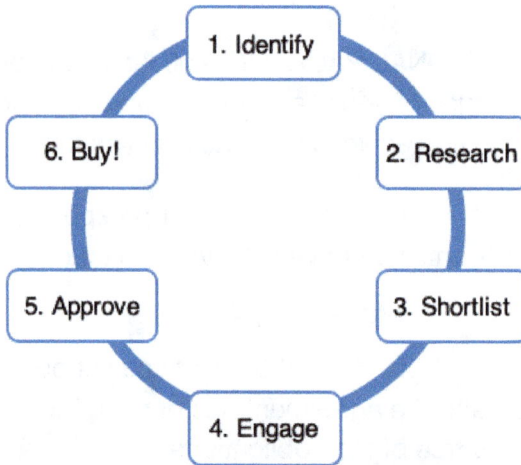

The Natural Sales Evolution (2013)

We can now capture a prospect's attention and start a dialogue about what their needs may be. In the example of the recruitment agency that has reduced its staff turnover to 15% per annum, my client who sells the recruitment tool, has the opportunity to post content about this result and the company's transformation and use it to grab the attention of their ideal prospects and start a dialogue where previously they wouldn't have been able.

By captivating this interest, they can help the prospect to realise they are fighting unnecessary challenges within their business that could easily be solved with professional support. Thus, they have created a new client.

Another change that you will notice is the introduction of self-implementation. In previous years, this would have been impossible with the only resources available being books or high-ticket price training course (which would have required an entire sales process to promote anyway).

"It is only when we have decided we can't do it ourselves and help is needed, that we choose to invest."

In the traditional buying journey, the identification of a need and the research around it would have been the point at which the decision to invest in a solution would have been made. There were no other options. However, in today's market, the decision to invest in a solution has now moved to much later in the process as more of us recognise that we can find what we need with free online materials. Before investing, we'll try and see if we can solve the problem ourselves.

It is only when we have decided we can't do it ourselves and help is needed, that we choose to invest. Previously, this would have been to Shortlist. However, if we do this process right, our prospect won't have a shortlist. Instead, they'll only have one person on their list of potential suppliers – us.

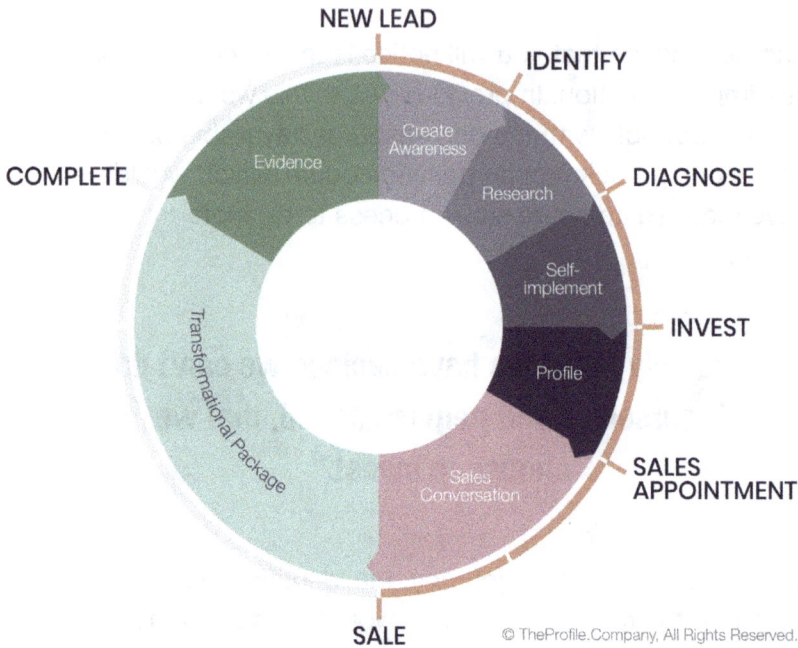

NEW LEAD

IDENTIFY

Create Awareness

Evidence

COMPLETE

Research

DIAGNOSE

Self-implement

INVEST

Transformational Package

Profile

SALES APPOINTMENT

Sales Conversation

SALE

© TheProfile.Company, All Rights Reserved.

If the prospect comes to learn about you during the Invest stage and is now comparing you to other potential suppliers, having great content that revisits each stage of the buying journey will help put you firmly at the top of the list. It will give them a chance to re-evaluate how they came to recognise they had a problem, if they've diagnosed the problem correctly, and if they can solve this themselves. If they revisit each of these stages, there is a strong chance they will now have developed a strong relationship with you.

In my model of the modern buying journey, I have also opened out the circle to show the complete journey of a prospect. The righthand side shows the modern buying journey, and the left-hand side shows what happens next. It reflects the transformational journey the prospect will go on with you.

With reviews, case-studies, and results being so critical, this too also needs to be reflected in the buying journey of

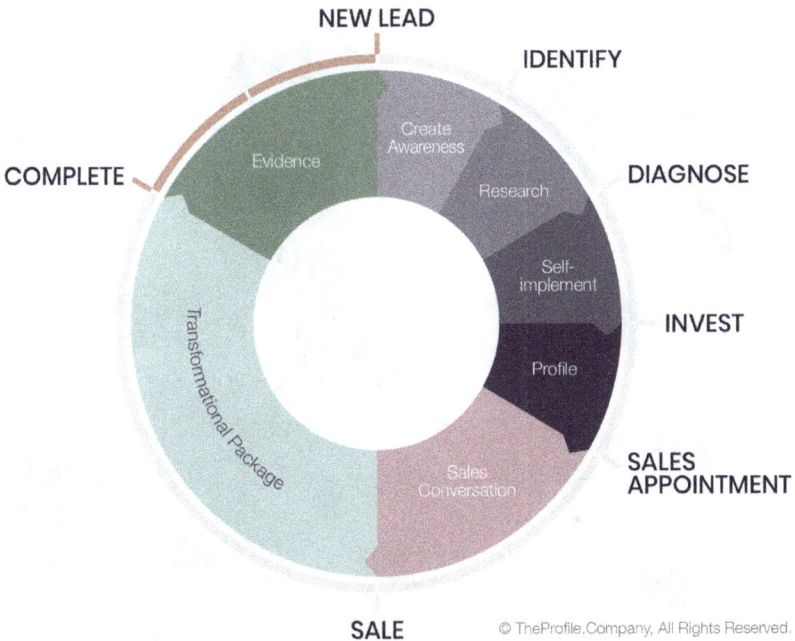

NEW LEAD

IDENTIFY

COMPLETE

DIAGNOSE

Evidence

Create Awareness

Research

Self-implement

INVEST

Transformational Package

Profile

Sales Conversation

SALES APPOINTMENT

SALE

© TheProfile.Company, All Rights Reserved.

our prospect. This is reflected in the diagram at 10 o'clock, as COMPLETE. Between 10 and 12, is

EVIDENCE. This is the time to collect case studies, testimonials and building your portfolio.

Between 6 o'clock and 10 o'clock, is the Transformational Journey. This is your package. The package that promises to take your prospect from where they are now to where they need to get to, as discussed in Chapter Two.

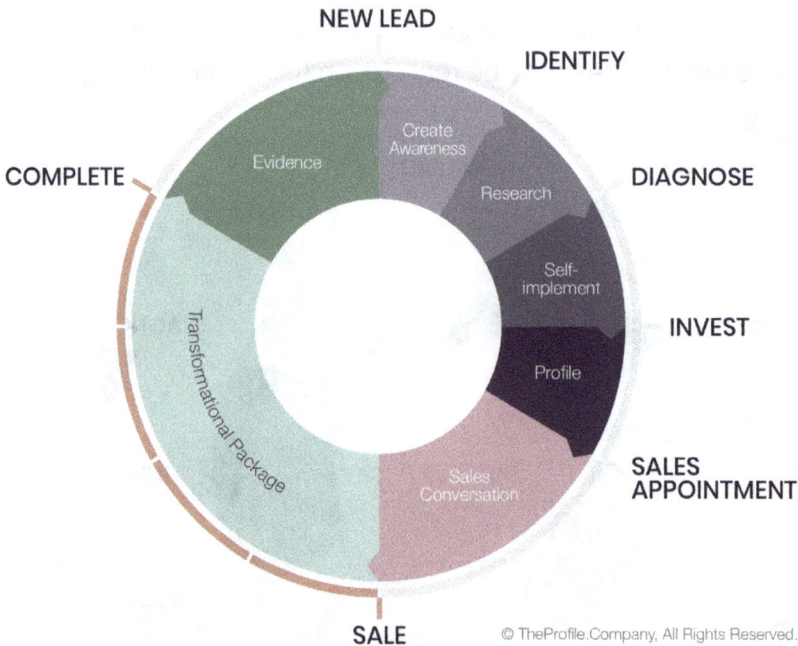

NEW LEAD

IDENTIFY

COMPLETE

Evidence

Create
Awareness

Research

DIAGNOSE

Self-
implement

INVEST

Transformational Package

Profile

Sales
Conversation

SALES
APPOINTMENT

SALE

© TheProfile.Company, All Rights Reserved.

You can see where these products sit within the buying journey above.

Each stage is absolutely critical. You may wish to continue with the clock diagram and write the milestones within your client journey on to the clock starting at 6 PM with the final one being 10 PM.

Between 6 o'clock when the deal is made, and 7 o'clock, you may like to detail your client onboarding process and create tools to speed up and simplify how you register a client. Tools like this form an asset within your business that new team members can follow, allowing you not only to make your business more efficient but also grow it.

As you create the milestones for your product, you'll also create helpful resources that will help you deliver your services, and your client achieve results. You'll be formalising your processes and writing down your methodology. Again, a vital asset within your business.

At this stage in your business, you may appreciate reading Daniel Priestley's best-selling book, "24 Assets".

10 o'clock is the moment you sit down with your client, review progress and agree that what you both set out to do together is now complete. You receive feedback and insights on the journey from their perspective and collect vital information for the case study and testimonials for your portfolio.

Working to The Buying Journey

Respecting the buying journey and understanding what your prospect is thinking and the type of information they are looking for at each stage will help you to create and supply the right content at the right time. Remember the example I gave when I was looking to lease a car, and each page of their website started with selling me on why leasing was a good idea? They had created all the right content but were supplying it in all the wrong places.

Ideally, you want to avoid posting content on social media that talks about features and benefits. This type of information is only of interest to those who are advanced in their buying journey. At this point, they will be on your website diving into your content to have their questions answered, and not on social media. Prospects interacting with you on Social Media are those that still need to understand why they need you and how you will transform their situation. Therefore, you want to avoid giving too much in-depth detail that the majority of people aren't interested in or ready for.

"Prospects interacting with you on Social Media are those that still need to understand why they need you and how you will transform their situation."

Instead, share stories about the industry, highlight companies that are getting things right, comment on why you think they are getting it right with insights that demonstrate your expertise, share articles related to your topic and write your own articles. Then, place your Call-To-Action - the invitation for the sales appointment - at the bottom of your post or article.

Creating Content Assets

One thing to note here is that you don't have to write all this content yourself, nor does it have to originate from your company. It is perfectly OK to share another person's content. In fact, they will thank you for it. You might opt to click 'Share' and make a quick remark on the quality of the article, or you might go a bit further and highlight individual sections and add your opinion too it. You may agree with the article or you may not; either way, starting a discussion about it is a great way to engage your audience and have them take notice.

Articles you share and articles you write are what I call Variable Assets. They act as free content that drawers the prospect into the conversation and can be used around the web to create curiosity.

A Fixed Asset, on the other hand, is a milestone piece of content that, more than likely, you have created. It is a quiz, a report, a book or a feature-length webinar, film or audio recording. It allows the prospect to spend extended amounts of time with you and get to know you. It is something they carve out time for and will support them in their buying journey.

Articles, short videos, and commentaries are variable assets because they tend to just deal with one topic, issue or symptom at a time. They are easy to digest and ideally should have a Call-To-Action at the end, inviting the prospect to engage with your fixed asset. The variable asset, the articles and videos, may be time-sensitive and in response to industry changes or what is on your mind that day. They tend to drop down in your social media feed, blog list or YouTube channel over time and not be so easily found. Hint: You can re-use this content and put into your Social Media rotation at any time.

Know What's Coming Next

With any content you write, it's essential always to have your eye on what comes next. What do you want your prospect to do as a result of coming to your content?

When we write it, we need to match the content to where they are in the buying process. This might be to speak of symptoms and justify the need to look at the issue further (create awareness), compare different solutions and approaches to a situation (research), or answer very technical questions to help your prospect complete something themselves (self-implementation).

It's important to know what your content is looking to achieve and include a Call-To-Action appropriate for the content.

> **"It's important to know what your content is looking to achieve and include a call-to-action appropriate for the content."**

An excellent example of this might be the car leasing company. Imagine if, at the early stages of my research, a quiz popped up saying that, by answering ten questions, I would know if leasing a car was the right option for my life and my financial situation. Would I opt-in for this? Absolutely. Based on my answers, the company could then send me to appropriate information.

If it concluded that I shouldn't lease a car, it could provide a quick article on how to buy a car, insure it and buy road cover (all with affiliate links to products I might buy as a result of making this decision).

If it concluded that I should lease a car, a great piece of content would be something that helped me to choose the right vehicle, the right provider, the right payment terms and understand the commitment I am making. Once I've consumed this, a call from a sales representative at the company would be very timely - if I haven't already called them myself!

Know the Problem You Are Solving

When it comes to selling your product or service, it's important to truly understand the problem you solve and how much your solution will benefit and transform your customer's life because, when it comes to pitching your service, people generally don't invest in solutions, they invest in solving problems. And the bigger the problem you solve, the bigger the paycheque.

This is why it is so important to understand your prospects, the business they are in, and exactly what they are struggling with. During the sales call, it's crucial to spend time delving into the issues and understanding what their problem is. Often, people are so busy with their lives and dealing with the status quo that they haven't even stopped to get present with the situation and understand the real impact their situation is having on their lives and their business results.

Once you've taken the time to help your prospect fully understand the extent of their problem, the cost of fixing it will seem like a small investment.

For my clients, the cost of having me write their LinkedIn profile isn't cheap, and I often avoid telling people the price before I've completed their Profile Review. This is because, without the ability demonstrate how their profile could be re-worked and how it will change their business, they won't perceive the value of what I am offering and therefore see it as an incredible investment. It is only when they get honest feedback on what is currently going on for them, and I show them what I can do for them, that they get excited and see it as affordable.

"In our marketing, we need to demonstrate our understanding of the prospect's problems and what they are trying to solve."

In our marketing, we need to demonstrate our understanding of the prospect's problems and what they are trying to solve. Presenting a solution, in isolation of talking about the challenge, is not going to win us any fans or position us as an expert within the industry we want to be in.

Last year, I met Andrew, a sales manager for a reputable car dealership. His main goal is to lease fleets of cars to companies. From a functional standpoint, this is what he does. He is simply ready to lease cars as and when a company identifies it has a need and is ready to purchase. There isn't much he needs to do other than

DANI JOHNSON

The bigger the problem you solve, the bigger the paycheque

meet businesses and let them know he is ready and waiting. If someone wants a fleet of cars, and they want this brand, they naturally come to him.

However, it appears this isn't really working. Sat on a major industrial estate, without a natural footfall, the showroom doesn't tend to attract a lot of visitors. He actively goes out to meet people and let them know he is there, and although the brand is highly searched online and his local dealership appears on location searches, not much is happening to engage with customers ahead of them deciding, independently, that they want this brand of car.

But is this true? Let me ask you. Andrew leases fleets of cars to people who need cars, but is this all he does? Or is he really responsible for helping Sales Teams get on the road and arrive at appointments in style? Isn't it true that the brand of car a salesperson drives and the condition of the vehicle reflect heavily on the brand of the company driving it? Isn't it also true that driving the right car will put the salesperson in the right frame of mind when arriving at a client's office and having the right vehicle in an employee compensation package is important for attracting new staff? The answer to all these questions is yes.

Therefore, Andrew doesn't just lease cars, and people don't just come to him for cars. They go to him to help them get their sales teams on the road, attract the right staff and build their own brands.

Andrew doesn't just solve the problem of giving them the right cars at the right price; he solves many problems for his clients. If Andrew wants to increase his business by becoming the go-to expert in his industry, all he needs to do is speak to his audience about these very real problems.

When a prospect arrives in his showroom, I am quite sure this is the conversation he will have with his prospect, and they will be grateful for it. What he needs to do, however, is get it online and start demonstrating this level of consideration and conversation in the content he shares.

The truth is, most people commissioned with the role of leasing cars for a company are not experts at it even if they have done it several times before. Leasing cars will only be one aspect of their role and not something they would do very often. The majority of people won't know what they are looking for, what questions to ask, what to consider, or what is important.

"The trick is to teach prospects how to buy our product, to share insights and ideas that they may never have considered before, and give them the space they need to consider it in their own time."

In many industries, this is why brokers exist; people who understand what to look for and will ask the right questions.

The trick is to teach prospects how to buy our product, to share insights and ideas that they may never have considered before, and give them the space they need to consider it in their own time. The more you do this, the more you'll be respecting the natural buying journey of your prospect and building rapport with them. They will see you as their Trusted Advisor. Someone able and willing to help them and someone who will respect them. They will no longer see you as a Salesperson they need to keep at arm's length just in case they get carried away and buy something they'll later regret.

For Andrew, there are multiple things he can write status updates about, write blogs or film short videos about and even write a book. A downloadable report outlining the things to consider when purchasing is an attractive offer for a prospect and, in downloading it, the company will be signalling to Andrew they are in the market to lease new cars. If he should then call the company to follow up, there is a high likelihood they will be grateful to hear from him, ready with their questions, something that would have been unheard of previously.

Andrew doesn't have to sit and pen the content himself. He can find content about compensation plans online (employee benefits, tax write-offs, talent brand), winning new sales (mindset, using travel time to learn, eating health, keeping the car clean and organised, arriving in style) and recruitment (prestige, brand etc.) and share it on his page. Although the articles won't relate to buying cars, when Andrew shares the article and writes the status update to go with it, he can write it in a way that shares his personal insights and draws the visitor to his conclusion. The visitor may or may not read the article. It doesn't matter. He's made his point, and he's helped his audience advance in their buying journey and gain confidence in making the right choice.

Handling Objections

The marketing system and materials you create can also be set up to handle and overcome objections your prospects are likely to have. For one of my clients, Adam, who is a highly respected solicitor, being able to win over his prospects and position himself as their trusted advisor and 'go-to' expert means having to deal head-on with his industry's reputation for over-billing. Adam is a specialist at resolving neighbourhood disputes, and his leading advice is to come to him as soon as a dispute starts and before lines are crossed that could negate the rights of the innocent party.

However, with upfront fees required for a consultation, many of his prospects will put off paying for advice in the hope the problem will just go away. It rarely ever does, and before they know it, his client finds themselves with a bigger bill than if they had come to him from the outset.

Thus, Adam wants people to come to him sooner rather than later. He wants people to avoid months of heartache and/or doing something that will later hurt their case. He also wants people to avoid the type of stress neighbourhood conflict can have on a person, as he knows from working with many people in this situation, a dispute can impact on all areas of a person's life.

What Adam wants is for disputing neighbours to come to him with their issue early, and view paying £80 for 30 minutes consultation a valuable investment. He also wants them to feel confident that they will get the answers they need within 30 minutes and won't end up staying for a full hour and leave with a bill for £150.

For Adam, there are many obstacles for him to overcome if he is going to gain new clients and serve them well.

Working on Adam's LinkedIn profile, we considered the mindset of the individual and built a system to overcome it. Instead of just asking the prospect to book a session and hoping eventually someone will, we first dealt with their objections.

When a person is distressed, they like to talk. When they need advice and input, they like to make sure they have shared everything about the situation. For Adam to provide the right advice, he needs to be confident he has all the facts correct. The type of information and detail a distressed neighbour is likely to get wrong and muddled over when talking to him, sending them well past the 30-minute consultation leading to high fees.

Therefore, we built in a system that allowed the person to fully explore their issue, note down significant events and the dates they occurred, and submit it ahead of the meeting.

By asking the prospect to fill in a form and take the time to write down the facts before the session, Adam has made sure he has everything he needs to provide the right information and advice within the 30-minutes session. This increases the chance of the neighbour feeling equipped to know what to do next within the agreed time and price.

In this example, Adam is charging for his initial advice, but even if he wasn't charging, the objection still needs to be handled.

It can be easy to think that because we are supplying free advice, a person will volunteer to spend time with us and not require convincing—however, the opposite is true. Your 30-minute free session is not free for the individual. Until you demonstrate the value and the urgency of the person speaking to you, that 30-minutes is expensive. We are all busy, and time is money. If a prospect doesn't consider the investment of time valuable or important, they aren't going to book a session.

> **"It can be easy to think that because we are supplying free advice, a person will volunteer to spend time with us and not require convincing—however, the opposite true."**

Several months back, I spoke to a company representative about GDPR. Like many, I was still in the dark as to exactly what the changes were and how I would need to adjust the management of my data to stay on the right side of the law. I asked the lady if she had a quick summary she could provide to help me ascertain how relevant the subject was to my business. I wanted the opportunity to evaluate its importance against all the other things within my business and make an informed decision as to whether I needed to prioritise it.

Instead, however, she invited me to a free half-day training session during which I would be provided with a full outline and could decide from there whether I needed their support. It felt like a massive commitment of time, if not a waste of time. Without knowing if it was relevant to me, I was unwilling to give up half a day of my time. It didn't matter that it was a free event; it didn't appear free to me as half a day out of my business is costly.

As a provider, we might be sure a prospect needs our services and offer free information; but it doesn't mean your prospect will agree with us or consider what we are offering as 'free' or valuable. Often, much work is needed to get the person to the same point as us and to tip the balance so they see our offer as valuable and something to invest time in.

The trick is to stand in our prospects' shoes and understand their position so we can make the path easy for them. When we identify their objections ahead of them telling us, we can create a sales process that easily navigates them to where they need to be. If a person isn't willing to travel to your event and invest half a day, it is probably because a vital piece of information is missing, either about who you are or the seriousness of the problem you're trying to help them solve.

"The trick is to stand in our prospects' shoes and understand their position, what they are thinking and where they are coming from, so we can make the path easy for them."

If people aren't taking up your offer to spend time with them one-on-one or attend a free taster event, then you'll need to do further work building out your offer. As you know, I offer reviews of people's LinkedIn Profiles, firstly because that is relevant to what I do and, secondly, because I recognised early on in my career selling

LinkedIn training that what people care about is themselves.

People are always concerned about how they look and how they are doing. Anything that diagnoses how well they were doing or makes it easier for them to pinpoint where they needed additional help would be of interest. It is why people love a good personality quiz or a diagnostic that reveals something about them, whether that is about their business or to tell them which superhero they are.

"A prospect doesn't want to book a Sales Appointment with you because they don't want to be sold to."

It is important to note here again that our outcome is to book Sales Appointments because, without them, there is no chance of achieving a sale. A prospect doesn't want to book a Sales Appointment with you because they don't want to be sold to. What they will book, however, is an appointment where they can learn something about themselves and their business that adds value. This appointment needs to be diagnostic in nature and help them identify if they have a problem and the extent of it. It needs to be informative and content-rich, but not *salesy*. It needs to lead a person to ask, 'so how can you help me?' It is only at this point we have permission to introduce them to our solution and ask for the sale.

With a compelling offer (Call-To-Action), it should be easy to book appointments with our ideal prospects. If it is not, and you're finding you are being turned down more than you are hearing 'yes', then you will want to re-evaluate your offer. If you are finding that people book appointments but then don't show up, again, you'll want to re-evaluate your offer. A good Call-To-Action should have people falling over themselves to attend an appointment with you.

Key Takeaways

- When you supply content at each stage of the buying journey, the person is building a relationship with you that will eradicate the competition.

- You don't have to write all the content yourself; you can promote other people's content with your own spin on it, positioning you as the source of good and helpful information.

- All content needs to fit together with relevant call-to-actions, so prospects move through the stages of the buying journey with you.

- You may perceive how big your prospects' problem is, but do they? This is why we have in-depth sales calls/diagnostics to help our prospect grasp the extent of their problem.

- When a person understands the extent of their problem, and its far-reaching impact, the cost of fixing it will feel like a small investment.

- Take the time to identify any possible objections your prospect may have and create content that answers the question, pre-empting the need to ask it.

- If people aren't taking up your offer of a sales appointment, it's because it isn't enticing enough. Review what you are offering and if it is a good exchange of time.

Engage

9. Engage

Now that we've fully appreciated how people buy and have begun crafting our LinkedIn profile and content to match, it is important that we now start to engage with our audience. (For full information on how to write your LinkedIn Profile visit www.TheProfile.Company)

Sitting behind our computer posting great content will not result in new sales on its own. Instead, we need to build our network and get known, so our name comes up in all the right conversations.

As we said at the outset, our goal is to have our most ideal prospects book appointments with us. To do this, we need to invite them.

In this chapter, we're going to review different ways to engage with our network, both online and offline, to fill your calendar with sales appointments.

Why Use LinkedIn

With 660 million users around the world, LinkedIn puts you on the superhighway to just about anywhere you want to get to. It's the number one platform for business and is the only platform where it is predetermined that the only acceptable conversation is business. It is not for online dating, socialising or posting pictures of your family or what you ate for breakfast.

It comes with its own code of conduct that is similar to business networking meetings. With your account and therefore profile, you are putting yourself into the most popular and most famous business directory in the world.

Your activities (posts, comments, shares) are highlighted to the people in your network, and their interaction with you are highlighted to their network, allowing you to leverage trust and gain access to just about anyone you want to be in business with.

And the great thing about it is that it's free. Not entirely as there are upgraded packages available, but everything I teach is free. At this stage of your business, while you're in 'hustle' mode, the free version has everything you need. Once you've perfected the basics within your business, the paid services offer additional services to help you ramp up your activities. Right now, however, we won't be needing them so your wallet can rest easy.

Although this chapter focuses on LinkedIn, it is worth noting that the ideas and principles transfer easily to most other platforms.

Respond to Comments on Your Posts

Make sure to check your 'Notifications' regularly to see who has commented, liked, or shared your posts. While only a small proportion of readers will leave a comment, it is worth honouring those that do by writing back, whether that is just to say 'thank you' or like their comment to you. Doing so will let people know that there is someone behind the screen that actually cares. Added to this, LinkedIn values this type of engagement and will bump your post into more people's feeds.

The best option, of course, is to try to begin a dialogue, especially if there is a topic or point of view that will gain a lot of interest from your network. Asking people to elaborate, answering questions or relating the topic back to something specific about that individual lets people know that you want to engage meaningfully in the content.

You may opt to invite the person to connect straight away or wait until the dialogue has progressed and it feels natural. You may find that the person has already reached out to connect.

If the conversation has been interesting or you've said something that has sparked their curiosity, there is a high chance they will visit your profile. It is at this point you have your chance to transform a LinkedIn connection (whether first degree or second degree) into a prospect. What you say on your profile is extremely important. Assume that the person has read your profile, and that is why they are connecting with you. This will allow you to move the conversation on faster and secure the appointment, and that you're talking to someone who genuinely wants to connect (if they aren't aware of your offer, they are clearly someone clicking random profiles to build their network).

The Profile. COMPANY

Would you like feedback on your LinkedIn Profile and expert journey so? Visit www.TheProfile.Company/Review to book a 30-minute one-to-one review with Naomi

When connecting with new people, make sure to write a reply before clicking 'Accept', so you are starting a conversation and engaging. It is good practice to pay attention to those who have commented, liked or shared your content so you recognise people who go on to invite you to connect and can say something more meaningful.

Reply to Connections

Often, people complain to me that they only receive invitations to connect on LinkedIn from people they don't know. They also tell me they decline the invitation, which, if you're doing everything right on LinkedIn is the last thing you want to do.

After all, if your profile pitches your business, looks professional and has a clear Call-To-Action, doesn't it make sense that someone connecting with you is interested in what you're offering?

For each new invitation to connect, it's important to take the time to respond. You can do this without accepting the invitation to connect by clicking on 'See all' in the top right hand of corner of your invitations. LinkedIn is always changing so if you can't see how to do it, click on LinkedIn help for guidance.

When responding, take the time to thank the person for the invitation and ask them why they are getting in touch. Do they have a question they'd like to ask? As your profile is clear about what you do, there is no need to feel awkward restating your call to action since there is a high likelihood this is what they want to be in touch about anyway.

A great time-saver is to create a template and have it easily to hand. Personally, I use TextExpander for Mac (PhraseExpress for PC). All I need to do is write a shortcode and the full message appears instantly on my screen. I will do it now and show you my response:

Hi (name), great to connect. Was it one of my posts, a comment or my profile that inspired you to connect? I'd be interested to know. If I can assist in any way, let me know.

Personally, I don't restate my invitation for a profile review in my message because not all connections are appropriate leads for my business. If I visit a profile and consider them to be an interesting lead, I might edit the message referring to what they do and make my offer. However, there is no real need to do this since, if a person is interested in it having read it on my profile, they will reply to the above message and let me know.

Personalised messages have the biggest impact; however, time doesn't always allow for this. If someone you don't know has reached out and they haven't added a note to the invitation to introduce the connection, and they don't look like a prospect, then consider how much time you're willing to invest.

From the messages you sent in response to the invitation, the probability of a person responding is about 10%. This is usually due to how regularly a person checks LinkedIn or their motivation to get in touch. A motivated prospect will respond immediately.

Saying that, early this year, I went back through 100+ invitations who hadn't responded to my initial message and sent a new message to ignite a conversation. There were several people who came back to me and apologised for not replying and restated their interest in working with me. Thirty-three people took up my offer to attend a free webinar (33%), and one person declined the webinar and bought a LinkedIn Profile from me instead. It was a profitable exercise.

As we've said throughout this book, the objective is always to get the sales appointment. Engaging with people and finding creative ways to start a dialogue, whether that be one-to-one or in a group setting, such as a webinar, is a valuable exercise.

The sooner you get off the platform and speak on the phone, the better! Because, as we already know, a sale cannot happen without a sales appointment and this is your opportunity to book them.

Accepting Connections

It's entirely up to you whether you want to accept all new invitations and it's worth considering upfront which strategy is best for you. If you're a salesperson working in another person's company, you may wish to only accept connections from people you have started a relationship with. Of course, if you have an established sales team that has invested in Sales Navigator, this won't apply to you since any new business-related connection will stay with the company.

When I worked for another company selling LinkedIn training, I was selective who I connected with. I connected with most prospects, especially those who had completed a LinkedIn Profile Review with me, but I didn't necessarily connect with everyone who sent me an invitation. Instead, I sent my message back (as outlined above) and clicked 'Ignore'. If the conversation developed, I would accept them into my network.

When I began my own company, I changed this policy. As an Expert and Trusted Advisor in my industry, I began to post more, and my goal was to build a following. Therefore, I now happily accept anyone who approaches me. I send my template message to each, but I don't mind if they don't reply since I know that they are now in my network and will see my posts. At some point, they might be ready to become a client, or their interaction with me might be seen by someone in their network who could become my client.

Personally, I am not a fan of building up a vast number of connections. I let my network build in its own time and aim to build genuine relationships with those that I connect with. It's a personal choice, and one developed around the nature of creating a time-sensitive service based on my expertise and ability to deliver.

Never Underestimate a Connection

When I launched my business, I made a simple status update on LinkedIn announcing the name of the company and my service. Several people 'liked' the post, including a prospect I had met the previous year. I had spent one hour with him outside Euston Station in London, pitching the business service of my previous company and how we might work together. We connected on LinkedIn afterwards and, as we both changed roles, we had no further contact.

However, this individual saw my status update and 'liked' it. Within a few hours, I received a number of messages to connect. I sent my reply message to each, and several people came back explaining they'd read my LinkedIn profile and wanted to speak with me about writing theirs.

One of these people was an ex-editor at the BBC who had now started his own communications agency. Within the week he and his business partner had become my first clients, many more new prospects and new clients have also come via this root.

So you see, it doesn't matter how little you know a person, it is always worth connecting with them as you never know who they are connected with, or who they will be connected with in the future, and therefore, where your next opportunity will come from.

Why we should always take the time to explain our process before the sale

Several months back, I recognised I needed to invest in a solution, so I called the first person I knew who provided it. She took my project on and got to work. A few days later, I attended a networking event where a new person independently identified my need and began guiding me through how to do it myself. He too was an expert in this area and a provider I could have turned to.

His explanation really helped me to understand how to go about things and what to do. I was so excited by his knowledge and ideas that I wanted to work with him. Only I was already committed elsewhere. I told him this and he gave me a few pointers to speak to my provider about.

The response I got from my provider was a brush off. It was awkward because I didn't want to appear to be telling her how to do her job or that she was wrong. However, the lack of insight into her process made me nervous and left me questioning her methods.

We didn't get any results from the campaign, nor did she conduct a debrief at the end to explain what she did and why we spent £600 on ads to achieve no new sales. From what I can tell, she didn't use any of the advanced methods the guy at the networking event talked me through and, to this day, I am convinced I didn't get the best service or that she is an expert in her field, and this is sad.

This is why we want to avoid simply saying 'Yes I can help' and jumping into the project. Instead, we want to take the time before the sale is agreed to talk about what is needed, why it is needed and our method. No matter how convinced someone is at the beginning of the conversation that they want to work with us, we still need to do due diligence and establish the right footing for the working relationship.

This step should never be overlooked. It's important that we do it correctly because every project we undertake reinforces our expertise and either provides evidence we can achieve results for our clients or leaves us and our marketing place wondering. Every client we take on is someone who may recommend us to someone else, or who might be called upon to give us a reference. "Fred, you worked with John, how was it?" We don't want to leave them floundering because they were disappointed with our work. When someone expresses interest to work with us, we need to revert back to the beginning of the buying cycle.

The Bank of LinkedIn

I often like to think of LinkedIn as a bank account that gains interest. The more money we keep in one bank account, the more interest we will incur. When we split our money across multiple accounts with small deposits, we receive less interest on our money.

LinkedIn is very much the same. When you segment your friends, family and colleagues into pockets of your life, very little magic happens. Prior to LinkedIn, and other social media platforms, this was just the way it was. You knew some people from the Tennis club, some from school, some from the university. There is your family, your cousins, your partner's family and their cousins. Everyone is in different pockets and other than weddings and funerals, they were unlikely ever to meet.

However, when you connect with each person on LinkedIn, you are bringing them all together into one place, and you will begin to see the most incredible connections. Several years back, I accepted a new friend on Facebook and realised we had six friends in common. Not only did I have no idea of this, but there was no connection between any of the six. They all came from different parts of my life, and what was more incredible, I had been a flatmate with all six individuals and so had my new connection, yet our paths had never crossed.

Of course, this is a very random example; however, if you're looking to get in touch with someone, you never know who knows who until you add them to LinkedIn.

My colleague Mike was once demonstrating the power of LinkedIn to a client and asked him 'Who do you most want to be in touch with right now? The guy said he had been trying for months to reach the CEO of a major company for a long time but had had no luck. A quick search revealed that his brother-in-law was already connected with the CEO. After calling him to enquire about their relationship and to ask if he could introduce them, he found out the pair were very good friends. He had absolutely no idea!

This is why you want to connect with each person you meet on LinkedIn. Your wealth really is in your network.

Add Your Call to Action

When posting articles, always make sure to add your Call-To-Action so people can identify how to get in touch with you. This might be to read an article, sign up for something, connect with you, or engage in the conversation by answering a question. If you don't have a call-to-action, it will leave people wondering if and how they should get in touch. As humans, we never like to do things that leave us vulnerable or at risk of looking stupid. Reaching out to connect with someone who might not welcome it or asking a question that isn't relevant to what the person is doing, might leave us feeling red-faced and is, therefore, something most people will want to avoid. With this in mind, we want to make it as easy as possible for someone to feel comfortable reaching out to answer their question.

Your Call-To-Action will depend on where the content sits within the prospect buying journey and what the appropriate next action is. You'll want to have this mapped out, so you know the Call-To-Action relevant to the piece of content you are sharing.

ROGER HAMILTON

Your wealth is in your network

Whatever action it is you want people to take next with your content, let them know. It might be to comment on the post sharing their thoughts, to watch your video, or book an appointment with you. It will all depend on where in the buying cycle, the item of content sits. We always want our content to call our prospect to the next logical step in the buying journey. We don't want to leave our prospects hanging and at risk of googling for their answer and finding your competitor.

You don't want to be leaving valuable business opportunities untapped.

Adding a footer to your posts is also good practice. It allows a person to learn more about you without opting to view your profile. A good post will capture someone's attention, but it doesn't mean their curiosity will peak enough to navigate off their feed to open your profile. A footer is a great way to cement in someone's mind exactly what you do and how they can engage with you.

Here is mine. It comes in at 796 characters, including spaces, which is a third of the available space. You may consider this takes up too much space and you may opt not to use it every time. However, consider that not many people read long posts, and it is better to make an impactful post with a clear call-to-action that backs up why you're an expert, than to use all the available space making your point.

🌸 *I am Naomi*

🌟 Write LinkedIn Profiles for people who are experts in their field who have a topic that is hard to explain and almost impossible to google and get the business foundations in place to make them the only person their prospects want to work with

➡️ If you're sharing content on LinkedIn to generate leads, you need to optimise your LinkedIn Profile or else your efforts will fall flat!

📈 Visit my LinkedIn Profile to take a 18-question quiz and discover if you have the right foundations in place to position yourself as the go-to choice for your prospects

Liked this post? *Want to see more*:

📝 Save this post

👉 Follow #LinkedInWithNaomi

🔔 Hit the bell icon on my profile for more content like this

💬 Ask me for a free #LinkedInProfile & Strategy Review.

📝 Save this post

🔝 Connect with me

Leverage Off-Line Networking

Ideally, we want to be connecting with each person we meet as we never know when it might lead to a powerful introduction. Gathering business cards and systematically connecting with each person on LinkedIn after a meeting or networking event is a basic practice. You'll, of course, want to make sure you personalise the message (or at least customise the template to the event), so people feel special and not just part of your collection.

Please note, at no point should you send an email pitching your services with a sales message to a new LinkedIn connection. While you can create a template message, it needs to build rapport and invite people into a relationship with you. Sending a sales message will violate your new social contract. At this point, the individual has done the equivalent of walking up to you at a party and asked what you do for a living. It would be highly inappropriate for the person to launch into a sales pitch that assumes you want to buy from them. Sending a sales message on LinkedIn in the first instance is exactly the same thing.

"At no point should you send an email pitching your services with a sales message to a new LinkedIn connection."

If the person doesn't respond for a while, it doesn't matter. Your status updates will keep you front of mind, and your LinkedIn profile will clarify what you do, and the individual will approach when they are ready.

The other week, I attended a networking event and listened to 100 pitches all before 8 AM, but twenty minutes later in a one-to-one conversation, I stared blankly at two people without a clue what they did. I couldn't even remember listening to their pitch despite being committed to being attentive to each person.

When they told me, I did remember, making it clear that I had listened, but I needed the prompt to re-engage with their message. When networking, it can be all too easy to assume that we have been heard and remembered, when the reality is, unless we are remarkable, it is unlikely that we will be.

Your profile is an important tool and, by connecting with people you meet at networking events, you will stay front of mind, and your audience will be clear on what you specialise in. With just 60-seconds to pitch your business, it is unlikely that you'll tell the full story or make the impact you could make if you had 10-minutes. This is why connecting after an event and having a well-crafted profile will make all the difference. It is your chance to back up what you said and pitch your business with more gravity.

Use LinkedIn to Develop the Conversation

Several months back, I attended a networking event an hour from my home. I had brief conversations with several people and followed up by connecting with them on LinkedIn. Four months later, I returned. Thanks to LinkedIn, several faces were still familiar to me. At one point during the morning, I went to get a drink when a guy approached me and asked how I was. He made a comment about recognising me and how my photo matched how I actually looked, which made me launch into a story about something that had happened the day before. I was only halfway through telling the story when he finished it for me. What I thought was an innocent observation was actually a cheeky comment referencing the status update I had made the day before.

At this time, I was a stranger to him. Yet, our LinkedIn connection had created a level of familiarity that had superseded and cemented our relationship beyond the time we'd spend engaging one-on-one with each other. We'd had no interaction other than this one time we'd met four months before, yet, we now felt familiar enough with one another to banter.

Get the Most from Off-Line Networking

If you're in any physical groups, get in the habit of connecting with each person you meet on LinkedIn, especially networking groups and training courses where sharing best practice and making introductions is the nature of the group. You will get far more return-on-investment (for your time and cost of attending) than if you just left the opportunity to meet at the event.

Even if you haven't met a person, it is still OK to reach out to them. Often, people sign up to networking groups with the full intention of attending but can't attend because something crops up. Or you may find that you didn't have time to meet everyone personally and missed out on meeting people you would have liked to.

In either case, reaching out on LinkedIn after the event is the perfect way to get the most from the event as there is a very high chance they wanted to meet you too. With the group in common, and your intention to meet, reaching out to connect on LinkedIn is a perfect and natural step. You may even ask for a phone conversation to replicate the time you could have spent at the event speaking. You are likely to find, especially if your profile represents you well, that they will be more than happy to jump on the phone with you.

Note, LinkedIn's algorithm is known to favour content visibility among new connections. When you connect with new people on LinkedIn, the platform is more likely to show your content to these new connections as part of its effort to enhance engagement and interaction within the network.

By continuously expanding your network and engaging with new contacts, you're not just broadening your professional connections but also significantly boosting the potential engagement rates of your posts, giving your posts the opportunity to make a first impression and engage a fresh audience.

Inviting People to Connect

When inviting people to connect with you, make sure to add a note to the invitation, as most people will be curious about who you are and why you are connecting. Don't rely on them to do the hard work; let people know why you want to connect and say something a little more than 'it would be nice to have you in my network'.

This is a tricky message because you also don't want to pitch your services too soon. Even saying what you do can hinder interaction. When someone reaches out to connect with me and tells me what they do and why we should connect, I will connect with them if I am interested in what they do, but I won't reply and start the conversation. I know that they are prospecting, and my take is that if they really want to draw me into their business, they should be the first person to respond. Thus, I don't send my template message.

> **"Don't rely on them to do the hard work; let people know why you want to connect and say something a little more than 'it would be nice to have you in my network.'"**

Getting the balance here is important. You want to say something that makes you an attractive person to connect with, but you also don't want to appear as though you're prospecting for business. This is why 'push' campaigns, where you're actively looking for business, can be tricky and why 'pull' campaigns, where you attract people to you, are so much easier.

Writing a note lets a person know you've taken care with the invitation, and you're not just trying to grow your network and your ego. It also builds the conversation, which is exactly what we need.

However, some methods of connecting could leave you unable to personalise your message. To avoid having your invitation shoot off before you've had the chance to personalise it, ensure you only invite someone to connect via their LinkedIn Profile using the blue Connect button.

This will guarantee you have the option to send a note. When you click Connect from a list where you can only see their name and headshot, the option may not come up.

"Writing a note lets a person know you've taken care with the invitation, and you're not just trying to grow your network and your ego. It also builds the conversation, which is exactly what we need."

Don't rely on your invitation message being seen, however. Sometimes, people will see your message and click 'Accept' before they have read it. While this will be in their inbox, they still may not navigate back to read it, especially if they have lots of messages. After your new connection has accepted your request, wait a few hours and, if they haven't replied, send a first message re-iterating your intentions.

Get Off the Platform

As soon as you have begun a conversation on LinkedIn, get off the platform. The sooner you move the conversation to a phone call or face-to-face meeting, the sooner you'll be winning new sales. If you believe the person is an ideal prospect, invite them to undertake your diagnostic (sales appointment) and avoid lengthy drawn out conversations. If you find yourself giving advice, you've gone too far.

To progress the call forward, simply tell the person that you're interested in what they are saying, and you'd like to help. Tell them it would be much easier to speak on the phone and then pitch your diagnostic call and invite them to book a time with you using your booking link.

"The sooner you move the conversation to a phone call or face-to-face meeting, the sooner you'll be winning new sales."

If you find a prospect is asking lots of questions or a question requiring a lengthy answer, simply write back and say 'It sounds like there is a lot here to discuss, why don't we jump on the phone and explore it? I am available at... / feel free to use this link to book a time in my diary'.

If you recognise the individual is an ideal prospect, but they haven't yet realised this, begin by asking questions that will help awaken them to a need and share an item of content that will interest them.

An excellent example of this is a LinkedIn Profile Review I offer within my business. If a person doesn't want to take me up on my offer, it is usually because they haven't yet understood the importance of a LinkedIn profile and therefore don't see speaking to me as a valuable use of their time. It is better not to push the point, but instead, continue to share good content on the platform that helps them come to an understanding of the problem and its value in their own time.

It is essential to keep a list of all your content including videos, blog posts and whitepapers, so you can quickly select the most appropriate item for each new person without spending too much time on it.

"If an ideal prospect says 'I can't afford it', always be willing to invite them to a diagnostic anyway."

Note, if an ideal prospect says 'I can't afford it', always be willing to invite them to a diagnostic anyway. If the statement is accurate, and they really can't buy, you will have at least helped them and probably won yourself a new advocate, someone willing to tell your target market about you. You may also find that now they understand what you do and the value you provide, they can afford you. This has happened to me so many times I can't count. Just be willing to come in service, add value, and take them at their word. If, at the end of the call, they still say the same thing, believe them. We're not here to pressure people.

Avoid offering to 'chat' to people or allowing yourself to become engaged in lengthy conversations that have no direction. All conversations need to be staged within the structure of a diagnostic. Otherwise, you are just wasting time.

Never allow a conversation to last more than 24 hours before inviting the person to a diagnostic. If you have too much back and forth, you're wasting time. There is little chance it will result in a sale. Only sales appointments do that. People are busy and easily get distracted, and there are only so many times you can follow up with someone. If the conversation lasts over several days, it isn't going to create the same energy and urgency as a quick discussion and inviting them to an appointment.

Remember we are all about the sales appointment. If you can't progress a conversation to a sales appointment quickly enough, consider why and be prepared to walk away. You may need to re-work your pitch for both your service and the diagnostic. Or you might need to consider the free content you are providing and why prospects aren't falling over themselves to have you solve their problems for them.

Exercise

Before moving on to the next chapter, why not take a moment to consider how you will apply the content.

Reviewing you previous answers and the last few chapters, what key information do you need to include on your Linkedin Profile? (About your believes, philosophy, experience, call-to-action, packages etc)

What areas of your live, have you not connected with people from on Linkedin? Who in your past could make a valuable connection?

Who are the main influencers and connectors in your industry that you should invite for lunch as soon as possible? i.e. test your new product ideas on

Key Takeaways

- Connect with everyone you meet, so you build your network.

- Reach out to people at networking events you didn't have the chance to meet, or that couldn't attend. People want to hear from you.

- Never pitch your message or services on LinkedIn unless you've been asked (but actually pitch the diagnostic first).

- Send a message to everyone who invites you to connect.

- Send a follow-up message if the person hasn't responded to a personalised message within a few hours of connecting.

- If you're inundated with non-ideal prospects getting in touch, move the gate posts. Too many leads is not the definition of a successful business.

- Add a Call-To-Action to all your content, telling your prospects the next logical step to take.

- Use LinkedIn to develop conversations but off the platform as quickly as possible. The sooner you move to a diagnostic (sales appointment) the quicker you will win new sales.

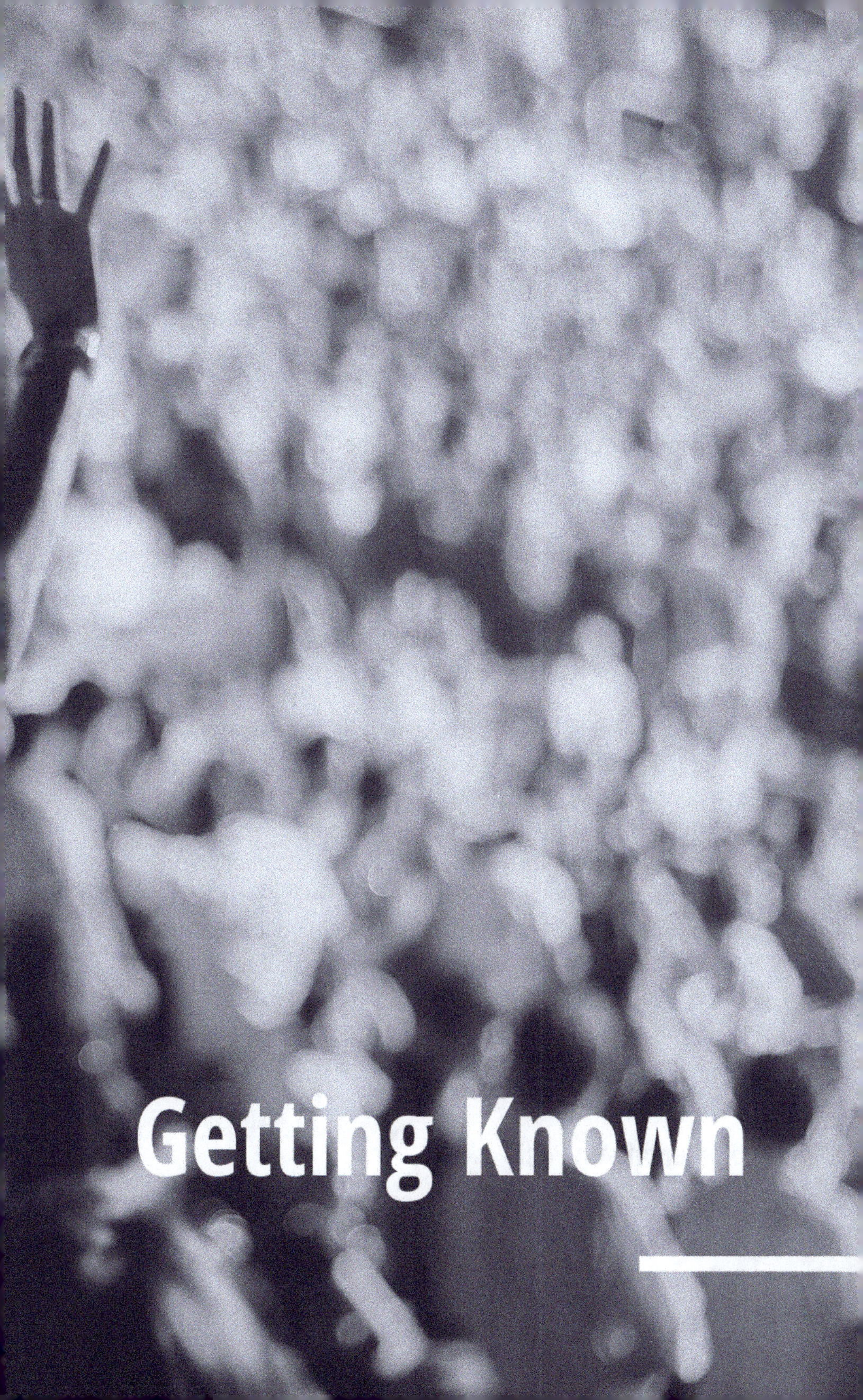

Getting Known

10. Getting Known

Now that you have a clear pitch, a valuable diagnostic and content to share, it is time to get known. There are many things you can do to win the attention of industry leaders and prospects that don't cost money.

In this chapter, we'll look at how you can use LinkedIn to build your network and book appointments with ideal prospects.

Remember, as mentioned before, LinkedIn's algorithms change all the time, and it's important to place the right emphasis on creating content. If you already have plenty of hot leads coming in from other sources, maintaining a content strategy may not be a priority.

In these instances, I advise avoiding creating a content strategy, as the posts tend to be bland and eventually have people tune out. Instead, wait until you have something to say. If you're attending 10 sales appointments a month, you will quickly have something to say, as each conversation will give you new insights and possibly, if there are misconceptions within your industry, things to get on your soapbox about. Posts that are written when you are fired up about your subject are far more likely to get a reaction from your prospects than if you're scheduling posts that have little energy in them.

Commenting on Posts

Engagement is everything. If you see a conversation taking place on LinkedIn and you have something to say, join in. Share your views and respond to other people's comments. If you read a blog that you enjoy, or absolutely disagree with, take the time to write a comment.

As you do, people will become curious about who you are and visit your profile. From here, there is a high likelihood they will ask you to connect. Once, a new colleague asked me how I get new leads. I said 'Easy'. I turned to my computer, found an active discussion thread and added an intelligent insight to the conversation. I turned back to him and said, 'Now we wait'. Within a few hours, I had several invitations to connect, most booked into a diagnostic call with me, and half became clients. I achieved this because my comment created curiosity, and my profile pitched my solution perfectly.

Commenting on blogs and status updates is also a great way to 'Pay It Forward'. We all enjoy seeing people engage with our content, and so, by doing it for other people, we pay it forward. We become familiar to them, and they are likely to return the favour later. Or it just comes down to karma. You just never know where the next lead will come from.

One day, I wrote a status update and a member of my local networking group 'liked' it. A few hours later, I had an invitation to connect which I followed up on by sending the template message (as discussed in the previous chapter), and we booked a sales appointment for later that day.

Sue became a client, and once I had completed her LinkedIn profile, I wrote a status update about it and tagged Sue in it. Within a few hours, one of my LinkedIn

Connections, Nigel, commented 'Oh, small world! I know Sue!' I wrote back 'not so small world'.

When Sue first approached me, I noticed that we only had one connection in common, Nigel, and Nigel had 'liked' my status update the same day Sue got in touch. Thus, I only knew Sue because of Nigel. Making the world small, but not that small!

Establish Your Position

We've already spoken about being consistent with your message and clear on what you stand for. To get known for your topic and stand out as an industry thought leader, we want to be sharing great content. You'll want to do this within your own feed as well as on your company page.

If you're an expert entrepreneur or small business, a Company Page is a vital asset as, along with placing your company logo on your LinkedIn Profile 'Experience' entry, it will also give you the ability to build followers and develop your message.

You want to think of your Company Page like an industry trade magazine. If you were to pick one up and review it, you'd see lots of articles on a wide range of subjects. All the articles are targeted towards a key audience and are subjects they want to know about. It is the quality and selection of articles that have people want to buy the magazine.

It's the same for your company page. In the majority of cases, people won't return multiple times to visit a company website unless there is something in it for them. You'll notice that companies with the biggest followings are those with popular products like Microsoft and Apple. When people visit these pages, they want to know about product updates and new launches, basically what is in it for them.

Therefore, when creating our page and putting time into the content we share, we need to keep in mind that people are always asking 'what's in it for me?' and make it clear. Ideally, we want to share a range of content on subjects that are relevant to our audience. We don't want to make it all about our company and what we are doing. We also want to vary our content, so even if the problem we are solving isn't front of mind, they still consider our page as the place to come and find helpful and relevant content that they'll enjoy, just like a magazine.

People won't come back to the page repeatedly to find out more about your company. A great way to look at this is to think about a trade magazine that costs £10+ a month. If you were to buy it, what would you want to see within it? If you were to pay this money and read every single article in it, what would you be learning? What would make you buy it each month and take the time out of your day to sit down and read it cover to cover?

When you share content, make sure you post your own editorial comment in the status and that it relates back to your core message. If it isn't immediately obvious, like some of the content we've suggested Andrew share, you need to make sure that your status is explicit in telling your audience how it relates back and why it relevant to your core message.

So how much of other people's content should you share, and how much should be yours? The general rule is 80/20. Your company page needs to be made up of 80% other people's content and 20% your own. This way, people will view it as a valuable source of information and not just a showcase for your company. Your company page needs to add value to the marketplace. People need to view you as a trusted and valuable source of information that is worthy of their time.

Your message is received even when it seems it is not

Last year on April Fool's Day, someone I know, who I'll call John, thought it would be a good idea to announce to his network that he was retiring. Of course, he was only joking. Unbeknown to him, though, the joke backfired. When people come to social media, they scan through many posts deciding what to read based on what captures their attention in any given moment. However, to decide not to read something, you first have to read it. As we scan-read, we pick up the key message and make our decision as to whether we want to read something thoroughly. Thus, the key point of every message is received, even if it isn't engaged with.

John's status update backfired because, as people scanned the content, they read his comment and began a quick succession of thought "Is John relevant to me? Is finding out more about his retirement important to me today and important at this moment?" If they conclude no, they'll move on, taking this information as fact and never realising it was a joke. They are unlikely to ever make the connection that it was April Fool's Day. Instead, when they think of his services and the possibility of working with him or referring him, they think "Ah no I can't, he's retired".

When writing status updates, be careful to say only what you mean and consider what a person will take away if they only scan read your post.

Of course, when sharing content, there are a few things to consider. As a Trusted Advisor, it's important to stay on topic and be consistent. We don't want to share too many posts that do not relate to our subject as we'll become known for topics we don't want to be known for, and this will only dilute our message and confuse people.

> **"Your company page needs to be made up of 80% other people's content and 20% your own. This way, people will view it as a valuable source of information and not just a showcase for your company."**

People only have a limited amount of attention and are quick to draw conclusions quickly. The wrong content could derail all your marketing efforts if your best referrers start concluding you've pivoted your business and begun focusing on other subjects. You'd be surprised how little it takes for people to assume this from seeing your content online.

Be Careful What You Share

When selecting other people's content to share, always read the content and assess the author. Decide whether you agree with the advice or not. If you don't, you can start a discussion by saying so. If you don't want to draw attention by offering a little criticism and controversy (which goes a long way for creating engagement, but isn't for everyone), opt not to share it. Remember bad advice will appear as your advice, so you don't want to be associated with it.

Before sharing, make sure to check if the article is associated with a sales funnel. If the content isn't about your subject directly, it doesn't matter so much if the prospect signs up to the author's mailing list and receives content from them. However, if the content is by a competitor, the last thing you'll want to do is send your prospect into the hands of your competitor. In these instances, avoid sharing the content altogether.

"Reading other people's content is a great way to become inspired for your own."

You can, however, use the article as inspiration to write your own content changing out the bits you don't like and adding in additional expertise or points of view that are uniquely yours or that you know your audience will appreciate. Note that I didn't say Copy/Paste. That would be plagiarism and very unprofessional. Plus, the automated systems of the online world will spot it and downgrade your content, limiting how much it gets shared.

Reading other people's content is a great way to become inspired for your own and, most of the time, you're likely to find that what you produce varies significantly from the content that inspired you.

It's also essential to make sure the source is credible. There is a lot of fake news out there and hyped up statistics that your audience may well see straight through. If they do, they will associate you as a person who doesn't know what they are talking about and is willing to share incorrect information.

We want to be known as a credible source who our audience can trust. There are several people in my network that I respect in this way. They just have to tell me to read a book, and it is delivered with Amazon Prime the next day. I value and trust their recommendation. We want to achieve the same with our audience.

Status Updates

Sharing updates on your day, new revelations, or ideas is also a great way to engage your audience, especially if you can share the credit with someone else and tag them in it. Status updates that tend to get the most attraction are those that celebrate others and their accomplishments. It is far better for you to champion your client's successes and feature them than it is to talk about yourself.

Pictures and quotes also get a lot of attraction with people liking and sharing them. One client of mine has made a habit of sharing her own quotes throughout the day in the form of a home-made graphic. As there is a consistency to the look and feel, it is easy to recognise her content in your feed. Over the course of a couple of weeks, she developed her brand voice and is now recognised for it. It has led to lots of invitations to connect and private inbox discussions that she then converts into telephone conversations with the opportunity to pitch her coaching services.

At the time of writing this, she is still firming up her packages and tweaking her sales approach. Each conversation she has tells her a little more about the types of people she is attracting, the kinds of problems they have and the solutions they are looking for. Each conversation is the perfect opportunity for her to practice her sales script and get feedback on her packages. It won't be long until she hits her goal, and the clients and money start rolling it.

When building your business, nothing can replace just getting on with it.

Tagging

Posts that tag colleagues and friends tend to get the most engagement. By typing '@' and then writing the person's name, you'll be able to select them from a drop-down list and tag them into your post.

It's essential to avoid doing this at random or manipulatively, though. If you haven't seen a person in a while and the post isn't relevant to them, do not tag the person as they will wonder why and probably not respect you for it.

A great way to engage your network is to highlight people who have added value to you and praise them for their contribution. Another great thing to do is post a picture at an event and tag fellow attendees in it. Say something positive about the event and/or group that everyone will want to get behind.

If you read an article or write one, and you're interested in a particular person's opinion, tagging them is a great way to draw their attention to it while inviting (indirectly) their peers to join in the discussion.

Hashtags

LinkedIn recommends a maximum of three hashtags with each post. When choosing them, you might opt to use the hashtags LinkedIn is suggesting at the bottom of the post. Or you can make up your own.

For this, you'll want to use a keyword associated with what you do. But, remember, only people who know they have a problem and are looking for a solution will use this hashtag in a search. Working with the psychology of how people buy and the buying journey, you'll want to select hashtags appropriate for the stage of the buying journey. For example, you wouldn't want to use hashtags using industry-specific keywords for content designed to create awareness.

You can also spread your net wider by finding popular hashtags your audience use every day. Put the keyword (plus the hashtag) in the LinkedIn search bar and see what results come up. By looking at the number of followers, you'll be able to see the number of people engaged with those words.

You might go for a hashtag that labels your audience, such as #coaching or #smes. Or you can delve deeper and find popular tags such as #conflict #annoyingclients for example.

You might also opt to use a hashtag as a way of filing and indexing your own content. Your audience might not use the hashtag, nor anyone else, but you can. When you search for the hashtag, your content will show, providing you with the ability to search your content based on a subject word.

LinkedIn advice is to only use three hashtags on any post. Hashtags can go at the end of your post or as a replacement of the word in the actual text. It's important here to make sure the text is still readable, and the hashtags don't detract from the ability to read quickly. Some people have a habit of tagging every word, but this makes it unattractive and hard to read.

Respect the Platform

When deciding what to post, it's essential to understand the platform and use it respectfully. I often refer to LinkedIn as an online business event and Facebook as going to a theme park. Whenever you consider posting a comment, a photo or sending a message to someone, ask yourself whether it is right for the environment.

Pictures of pets, family members or your dinner are frowned upon on LinkedIn because it is a business platform; a business environment and not the place for this type of conversation. If someone approached you at a business event and started showing you cat pictures, you'd think it very strange. Whereas if you were talking to your friends in the pub and they started showing you cat pictures, you'll just see it as part of being in a friendship.

How you would show up at a Business Event is exactly how you want to show up on LinkedIn. If you wouldn't attend a networking breakfast in your wedding dress, don't show up in your LinkedIn profile picture in your wedding dress.

"If you wouldn't attend a networking breakfast in your wedding dress, don't show up in your LinkedIn profile picture in your wedding dress."

Facebook, on the other hand, is different, and it is essential to respect the various reasons people are on the platform. In the small business arena, it is normal that our Facebook feed and usage is a mix between business and personal. However, for many of the people we sell to, there is a high likelihood that they are employed, and Facebook is a personal tool. They won't appreciate being approached about work-related subjects in their personal domain.

Facebook is like similar to a theme park because if you were to spot a prospect in line for candy floss with her family, the last thing you would do is walk up to her and start a conversation about work and whether you can help them. You immediately know this would be inappropriate timing. They are there with their family. If you did walk up to them and start talking business, they would likely be very unhappy about it and not your call on Monday morning.

If, however, you spot them, say hello, enquire about their children, the rides they've been on and if they are enjoying themselves, and leave it at that, you will have made a new friend and deepened your relationship with your prospect (by the way, this would be one of your locations in the 7-11-4).

Just as you should respect a prospect on their personal time, you also want to respect them on their social platforms.

"If doing something doesn't feel right or comfortable to you, it is probably the wrong thing to do."

I always refer to it as a social compass. If doing something doesn't feel right or comfortable to you, it is probably the wrong thing to do. Online relationships follow the same patterns as offline relationships. This is why we get annoyed when a new connection sends us a message pitching their service and telling us the benefits of it before they have taken the time to get to know us and respect the new relationship. When a message is sent too soon, it violates the natural progression of building a relationship and doesn't respect the individual.

TAKE THE SCORECARD

Discover how well your business measures up against the strategies and insights discussed in this book by taking our scorecard.

Upon completion, you will receive a complimentary one-page business planner that encapsulates everything covered in the book and evaluates your performance across these critical areas.

The planner is designed to provide a concise overview, aiding you in identifying strengths and areas for improvement, ensuring your LinkedIn strategy is as effective as possible.

Go to **http://www.theprofile.company/scorecard**

Key Takeaways:

- Engage with your audience by commenting on status updates with insightful tips and insight that grab people's attention and will position you as their expert.

- Consider your company page to be like a trade magazine and share content on subjects relevant to the problem you solve for your prospect. The content doesn't have to always be your own. A magazine is made up of multiple authors.

- Write a status update with the content you share giving your own editorial on why it is relevant to your target market and if you agree or disagree with it.

- Be consistent with your message and your brand, so your audience recognise you for it.

- Respect the platform and the people on it. Understand this is a business environment and show up as you would in a networking meeting.

- If you wouldn't do something offline, don't do it online. Know the difference between 'feel the fear and do it anyway' and poor judgement.

Making it
Happen

11. Making it Happen

So how do we take this from being another theory in a book to reality? Well, my best advice is *just get started*. You'll never have everything finalised, as a business is an ever-evolving entity. Plus, until you start speaking to potential clients and working with them, you won't have all the necessary distinctions and insights needed to 'finalise' your offering.

The key to making your business a success from the outset is to offer transformational results. If you believe in what you do and that you can deliver your client's from where they are now to where they need to get to or are at least dedicated to staying the course until they do, you're in the right place. This type of promise will have your prospects buy into you, and you will avoid crippling under the pressure of having to assure people that you know everything, and everything will be perfect.

> **"Being an expert is not about having all the answers, but rather about having the right level of knowledge, experience and intuition to navigate any situation that arises and deliver a result."**

When you deliver transformational results, you gain evidence that demonstrates to prospects what you are capable of. Told well, as a story, and you'll soon find your clients and prospects pitching your services brilliantly to your future prospects.

When you begin, your transformational results might be small but, as you gain more distinctions and experience, this will expand and so will the solutions you offer.

The worst thing you can do is lock yourself away, promising that, once you've written all four modules of a course, you're going to market it. This method will just send you broke. Great products are only to be built when you are working in tandem with clients. If you can't sell the product by pitching it now, you certainly won't be able to sell it after you've invested hours of time and money creating it in isolation.

"If you can't sell the product by pitching it now, you certainly won't be able to sell it after you've invested hours of time and money creating it in isolation."

Give yourself the gift of flexibility by only starting to work on a product when you have real people ready to buy it and digest it. This way, you'll be able to ebb and flow, twist and bend until you craft the perfect product based on real feedback and interaction with your ideal market.

Taking your product to market now, while it is still an idea, is the best and most sensible way to run a business. You may feel a pressure to deliver after your prospect says 'yes' and becomes a client, but you know you can deliver otherwise you wouldn't have created it. With the right planning, you'll create a great first product with nothing to worry about.

Let LinkedIn Get You Started

Getting started on LinkedIn is the perfect way to begin your business. LinkedIn removes the need for a fancy website, expensive branding and perfect words. When your business is new, you won't know how your website should look or what it should say. Trying to complete it before going out to the market and testing your ideas will be a waste of investment. Waiting for it to be finished will only delay you. Getting started with just your LinkedIn profile and activity will allow you to focus on getting results for your clients and perfecting your product.

Once you have something worth investing in, you'll see a return on investment for your website faster than if you waited, and you'll create branding that is spot on for your marketplace. Anything else is flying blind.

The wonderful thing about LinkedIn is that it gives you the freedom to edit and tweak your profile whenever you need, with absolutely no cost or technical knowledge. It also puts your business pitch at the forefront, out in the real business world where your prospects spend time.

Plus, you can draw attention to yourself and market your business by posting content and engaging with your network for free. You can even search for your most ideal prospects and see who they are connected to and reach out, or better, ask for an introduction.

In the early stages, there really is no better tool than LinkedIn.

Start with your Profile

As we've mentioned, a person will only book a sales appointment if they see it as a valuable investment of their time. If you are active on LinkedIn, posting updates, publishing blogs, sharing content and commenting in discussion threads, then you'll want to make sure your LinkedIn profile clearly pitches your business and invites people to a diagnostic session with you. If it doesn't, you're missing out on vital opportunities to get known and speak with your ideal prospects.

You'll only ever be as successful as your pitch, and without a good LinkedIn profile, you're definitely making life harder than it needs to be.

To create your profile, check out my book What to Put on Your LinkedIn Profile and my website www.TheProfile.Company.

Here, you'll find plenty of information, tips and insights on how to build out your profile. You can also download my Entrepreneurs Ultimate Guide to Writing a LinkedIn profile that comes with a LinkedIn template (see the back of the book for resources)

Would you like feedback on your LinkedIn Profile and expert journey so? Visit www.TheProfile.Company/Review to book a 30-minute one-to-one review with Naomi

ANTONY ROBBINS

If you add value, you will become your brand. Find a way to add more value than anyone else.

Stay True to Your Message

It can take time to get known in your industry but, if you are consistent with your message and what you stand for, it won't take long for you to get known as an expert in your industry and for your influence to grow.

The worst thing you can do is continually change your business niche and the problem you solve, confusing your audience. I know a few people who have made a big bang with their business and quickly become known as the 'go-to' expert within it, only to completely change what they're doing within a few months. This leads to confusion and will eventually lead to people not wanting to refer business to you since they won't know if you'll be happy to receive the referral or if you can be trusted with their contact.

It doesn't matter if your packages and services change over time, because people will expect this, as evolution is a natural part of business. The difference is staying clear on the problem you solve for your clients and why. When you lead with this, building your business is much easier, and it gives you the flexibility you need to grow.

Get off the platform

Success on LinkedIn is not about being on LinkedIn. It's about leveraging the trust in your network and developing relationships, so people want to discuss their problems with you. This can happen online and offline. LinkedIn is all part of the mix. The key is to always have your eye on booking sales appointments because, as we've said, sales appointments are the only way we get sales. And winning new sales is why we're working on LinkedIn in the first place.

Some of your relationships with prospects will start on LinkedIn, and some will start off the platform. Either way, it doesn't matter as long as you are booking appointments and posting content that impacts your marketplace - helping ideal prospects go from not knowing they had a problem to realising they need to invest with you immediately - you're doing great.

LinkedIn is the perfect way to get known and heard within your industry. It backs up everything you are doing offline and gives you the ability to share your message far and wide daily for free. It is an international superhighway where people are looking to connect and exchange for the betterment of others. Plus, you can take the content and most of the strategies you learn here to your secondary platforms, such as Facebook and Twitter, as the same principles apply.

The more active you are, the more likely you'll be invited to speak at events, guest blog, and attend influential industry meetings.

A few weeks back, my client, Sue, received an invitation to connect from a 2nd-degree connection who had just seen her latest post via a mutual connection who had commented on it. The new connection immediately invited Sue to speak on a panel at an upcoming event with other prestigious individuals because he had been impressed by her LinkedIn profile. He liked her original voice and her message.

Remember to always focus on filling your diary with a sales appointment. Without this firmly set as your intended outcome, you'll be 'networking' but 'not-working'.

Create Real Results

Building your business is time-consuming and often 'all-consuming'. We have a lot to think about. From learning to run the business, winning new business, managing our time, there is one thing that can't be forgotten, and that is creating transformational results for our clients. The type of results people will talk about.

For this, we need to stay focused on the end result and what we're delivering. Our business isn't about working the hours we're contracted to work, but rather, staying until the job is done because you promised to deliver a result.

Building with finesse

Being an expert isn't about having all the answers or knowing slightly more than anyone else. It's about having the experience to know how best to handle challenges and unexpected hurdles and being able to navigate around them successfully. Something no one can learn from a book.

It can take years to build this level of experience.

In the early days, it may be hard to find paying clients as you build your network and develop your pitch and product offering. The key, however, is to avoid locking yourself away to focus on developing more marketing content that isn't converting into sales. Instead, it is better to focus on building relationships with those in your network and offer to help people whether you get paid or not.

It may seem counterintuitive, or that you are underselling yourself, but the truth is, until you have proven results, it can be hard to get paid assignments. Working with a client on a live project will give you more insights and distinctions about your marketing materials and how to achieve results and create attractive packages than another activity you invest your time in.

The last thing you want to do is become known as an 'expert' within your industry and be nothing more than a puff of smoke. The entrepreneurial world is sadly saturated with people claiming to be able to transform your life with their magic beans yet fail to make the slightest impact on their clients' lives. Being photographed with famous individuals and shouting loudly does not make you a credible expert. Results do.

To get yourself started, focus on creating transformational results for your clients that people will talk about. Build your expertise, and the rest will follow.

Booking Sales Appointments

I think I may have hammered this point to death now, but there is nothing more important than getting in front of your prospects and talking to them. Even if they don't buy from you, what you learn in these conversations will be invaluable and aid you in all future conversations.

Our promise is to deliver the result, not just a service

Several years back, a new colleague asked me how I had spent my afternoon before our meeting. I told her about a phone call I'd made to a client and how I walked them through a challenge they were having implementing the training with their staff. Her first response was to ask if we were getting paid for the phone call. I told her 'only in as much as he bought a training package worth £4000 a few months ago. So in my view yes'.

However, her opinion was if this additional time wasn't written in the proposal as part of the initial cost of the training, this extra time was not allowed. That, once we'd left the training room at the end of the day, if the client couldn't figure out how to implement it, he was on his own. Personally, I couldn't have disagreed more.

Our client was grateful for the extra 30-minutes I provided and the help I gave. From my point of view, I had sold a package to take the client from where they were to where they wanted to get to, and my work wasn't done until they had achieved it. This wouldn't be a perfect science of course, as with any training, it is subjective, but I could at least spend time giving pointers to get them moving forward.

And this is what it means to be building a business as an expert. It means staying with the client until they have achieved the result we set out to achieve.

You don't even have to know exactly what you're offering and how. You'll learn this on the road as you go.

When I began my company, I offered LinkedIn Profiles. The more profiles I did, the more I understood my target market and what was going on for them and could create further products to support them.

When I sold my first six-month coaching package, I simply pitched it over the phone and summarised it in an email. When I pitched my new solution to my next prospect, I copy-pasted the email and used it again to make the sale. After this happened several times, I started to spot I was onto something. It was then that I wrote the sales page and placed it on my website.

My first prospect did ask 'is this on your website?' But previous experience had taught me it wasn't that he wanted to see it as an official product on my website to believe it, but rather, he needed to see it written down to commit to it.

"My business will tell me what it wants because my business is my clients."

Once I began making sales of the product and working with my clients, I knew I had something worthy of investing in. That coaching package is now the cornerstone of my business and has become so much more than what it was in that first email.

If it had been the old days, my hardship days that my first book Grassroots to Green Shoots is based on, I would have spent a week writing a fancy brochure and webpage, isolating myself at home trying to perfect it while having no interaction with my target market. If you know about my book and what I talk about in it, you'll know that this method nearly bankrupted me.

It is only when we get out and talk to our prospect that we can understand them, what they need, and what they are willing to pay for. The more time you spend with your clients, the more of an expert you will become in their problems – and this is exactly what you want to become as it is only by knowing their problems that you can become an expert in solving them.

> **"The more time you spend with your clients, the more of an expert you will become in their problems."**

For me, writing LinkedIn profiles as a core product was not a sustainable business. I knew that, but I started anyway. I didn't sit at home and try to figure it all out first. Well, in my story, I had no choice. I had to get selling or get a job. I constantly said to myself, 'My business will tell me what it wants because my business is my clients'. Sure enough, they spoke, and, within time, I had my full product eco-system in place and the foundation for good earning potential.

Stay Front of Mind with Great Content

Talking about the problems you solve and the results you achieve for clients will help you stay front of mind. People love to 'like' success stories and especially those about the results you've achieved for your clients, as opposed to your results that can come across as self-promotional and, perhaps, arrogant.

Great content and being active on the platform will have you stay front of mind with your audience and your name coming up in all the right conversations. What we share will reinforce who we are and what we're up to. Sharing photos of you speaking at events, stands at an expo, and your new marketing materials, will all reinforce in people's minds that your business is active and busy.

The best way to create your own content is to turn what you learn into content. As an expert in your industry, I am going to assume that you continue to read about and study your subject and stay on top of industry news. This is the 20% I mentioned earlier. You want to spend 70% of your time delivering transformational results, 20% of your time studying to remain an expert (Sales Appointment and reading/watching etc), and 10% moving all the pieces around). As you spend time learning more about your subject, something you probably do without even realising it, why not turn it into status updates and blog posts?

Keep a highlighter handy and highlight key concepts and ideas you could create a status update out of. When you leave a sales meeting, create an audio note to capture your thoughts and the energy you feel so you can re-create it when its time to sit down and write a post (or why not do a live post right there on the street? – if that fits your personality).

Confidence Creates Content

When you are absolutely adamant that the problem you solve has to be solved your way, you'll get out of your own way and show up in your marketplace the way you need to - to have an impact. It can be easy to question ourselves and stay quiet; yet, if we know what we are talking about and want to save people from suffering unnecessarily, we will shout loudly. Just as if you saw a child about to walk into the road, you'd jump up and stop them. It's just the same with publishing good content.

When we are passionate about what we do and passionate about stopping people living in pain, we'll have no choice but to step up and say something. We'll jump up from our seat and shout without a thought for ourselves or how silly we might look. Ultimately, we get out of our own way. We stop worrying about ourselves and the things that don't matter, and our lives become about serving our clients. Before we know it, we're months into our business, delivering excellent results and wondering why we ever doubted ourselves.

> **"When we are passionate about what we do and passionate about stopping people living in pain, we'll have no choice but to step up and say something."**

Great content is just this. The types of posts that have you shouting 'stop' to your audience and building a clear case for why they need your help now, and why they need it solved your way. It's this type of passionate writing; the times when you don't hold back - that pulls a punch and has you forget about yourself and your ongoing internal conversation of self-doubt and self-worth (which, by the way, – we all have!).

When we show up like this, the world shows up to hear us.

Remember, LinkedIn isn't like traditional PR. You don't want to be writing 'safe' posts and only make announcements about the company. Instead, you want to create engaging content that gets people talking. When you do, you'll be a thought-leader and a trusted advisor to your prospects. Of course, avoid being offensive, negative or outright criticising people as this will never do you any favours.

Just Be You!

From my observations, there has never been a better time in history than right now just to be you. It seems that, everywhere you look, we see people succeeding just by being themselves - and who knew? A few years back, I tuned in for the final episode of Celebrity Get Me Out of Here and heard Gogglebox star Scarlett Moffatt say "I can't believe I made it to the final! If I win this, it'll prove that just being yourself is all you need to do - who knew that just being yourself was enough!" I couldn't have cheered more. In fact, I downloaded the app and voted for her. It doesn't appear that it is just Scarlett waking up to this message, it seems that there really isn't a better time than right now just to be you!

"There really isn't a better time than right now just to be you!"

To be you, you just need to show up and come in service to others. As we just outlined, being passionate about solving a problem and saving people from unnecessary suffering is enough. When we do this, we put others first and relate to people in a way that makes a difference. We are genuine and authentic, and people buy into us.

If you have built a robust sales process with a compelling call-to-action, and deliver transformational results, there should be no reason why these strategies won't work for you.

Getting Started

Remember you don't need to have all your ducks in place to get started. You simply need to get started. You need to start speaking about your solution and the problem you solve and get known.

Your message will evolve, and so will your offering, so there is no reason but to get out there and do something. You can't wait to have everything in place before you do because, until you start pitching your services and getting a response from your marketplace, you won't know if you have anything interesting or valuable to offer.

Until you start working with your clients and providing them with a transformation, you won't know the distinctions needed to guarantee a result. And you don't need all this figured out before you start because your new client won't be buying into your system and process, they'll be buying into your passion for the solution and your commitment not to stop until you've achieved a result for a client.

Spending Time Online

Using social media platforms, especially LinkedIn, to get known is a fantastic thing to do. But how long should you be spending online? The industry quoted amount is 9 minutes a day or 45 minutes a week. I would agree, however, add a deeper level of thought to this. Merely being on the platform without direction is of no consequence at all. We can all sit there, click around and waste 9 minutes on activities that don't add up to bringing in new business.

Instead, I recommend focusing on your outcome: getting sales appointments and then investing the right amount of time per day, week or month to ensure your appointment diary is full.

Key Takeaways

- Until you start speaking to potential clients and working with them, you won't have all the necessary distinctions and insights needed to 'finalise' your offering.

- Your dedication to stick with a client until they have achieved a transformational result is the only promise you need when starting out. It will remove the crippling pressure of having to get things right first time and having all your ducks lined up.

- Never lock yourself away creating products. Instead, get out there. Meet your prospects, design your solution with them and create as you are delivering it – so you're actually getting paid!

- Instead of focusing on marketing content, focus on having conversations with your marketplace and begin solving small problems for people whether you get paid or not. It will give you the insights and inspire you to create content people want to read.

- You're an expert on your subject and study it naturally. Turn your studies into compelling content that educates your marketing place. By writing posts and status updates, you'll take your understanding of the subject to a deeper level than if you just wrote notes on it.

- When you put your customers' problems first, your business will tell you what it needs.

- Become an expert in your prospects' problems.

- You don't have to have all the answers or the perfect solution to get started, you just need to start.

Momentum

12. Momentum

Reading all of the above, it can feel overwhelming. Having been an entrepreneur for over fifteen years now, I know just how hard it can be, both mentally and emotionally. But I also believe, one of the biggest drains on us is feeling guilty about not doing what we think we should be doing.

It's great to read books like this, and a thousand others like it, to get a good sense of what we should be doing, yet half our pain after reading them will come from NOT implementing what we learned.

Knowing what to do - or what we want to do - and not doing it can put us in a continual state of stress. Often, there just aren't enough hours in the day to accomplish all that we know to do. The result is feeling like we're continually lagging behind and stalling.

"Often, there just aren't enough hours in the day to accomplish all that we know to do. The result is feeling like we're continually lagging behind and stalling."

However, despite feeling this way, we have to give ourselves a break. One thing I have learned is that things will happen in their own time. Often, I know what to do, yet doing it doesn't come naturally. I have found that, when things don't happen easily, it is because they aren't ready.

For example, last year, I finished producing my online course that accompanies this book and helps implement everything taught here. It gained fantastic reviews and results for clients. My intention was to run monthly introduction sessions for prospective clients to attend and sell places on the course. However, despite setting dates for the sessions, nothing happened. In fact, I don't even know what happened to the dates I set. I just know that they didn't happen.

> **"Often, what we resist isn't laziness, procrastination, or any other negative label we've been taught to give a lack of progress, but rather a timing issue."**

What did happen, however, was that I said 'yes' to the opportunity to host an event with Key Person of Influence co-founder Daniel Priestley in the city I live. It was a massive challenge, and one that took a lot out of me. Over the months cultivating the event, my message became a lot clearer, this book got its title. Having run this big event and built an audience, hosting the monthly events felt natural, and the first ones have taken place without a hitch, with attendees enthusiastic about signing up for the course.

Often, what we resist isn't laziness, procrastination or any other negative label we've been taught to give a lack of progress, but rather a timing issue. The project just isn't ready yet. I spoke about writing this book for a year before I actually put pen to paper. I wrote the online training course as a way of forcing the book to take shape. Then, I spent four months trying to craft the book from the course, only to realise it wasn't happening because it wasn't ready.

Once I had the name, I was halfway there, but still, nothing happened. Then, one weekend, I read a book that inspired me, and before I knew it, I had sketched the book outline within 10 minutes, and in two half-days of writing, I wrote the first draft of the entire book. Please note, the book doubled in size during the second edit and took a while longer to edit.

Thus, I am an advocate for focusing on the destination with absolute commitment and clarity and doing what feels natural and achievable. I call this intuition; you might call it something else. When you get good at knowing when to move and when not to move, you start seeing everything fall into place and, when you look back, you'll realise your life has transpired with perfect synchronicity and timing. There was nothing to worry about. And, as you begin to trust life, the stress disappears.

I know that, within my business, I am not doing everything perfectly. I also know that I often drop things and don't have all the plates spinning all the time perfectly, but I also know that I am getting better at it. I also know that, despite feeling that I am lagging behind on a few things, I am advancing quickly in other areas. I also know I am making excellent progress with the resources available to me. Someone else might be able to go faster if they had a better mindset or more financing, but that would be them. This is me.

With my eye continually on the bottom line, I am always aware of the new clients I need to win and what is involved. It is a constant balancing act between doing what I need to do to keep the business afloat, developing new ideas to grow the business, and delivering results for my clients. In many respects, client work is like having a part-time job. That might be a strange thing to say, as they are my work because, for every moment I am fulfilling on contracts, I am unable to do sales and win new business or develop new projects, just the same as if I did take a part-time job working elsewhere.

"It is a constant balancing act between doing what I need to do to keep the business afloat, developing new ideas to grow the business, and delivering results for my clients."

Realistically, development within our company may be restricted to just one day a week if we have four days of client work. It's a sobering truth that few of us calculate that when chastising ourselves for the lack of progress or comparing ourselves with others.

This being the case, we can soon start to understand why we might not be progressing as fast as we might like, or why feeling guilty about not implementing everything we need to do might be a waste of our precious energy. Instead, we need to stop and congratulate ourselves on actually winning the client work that is consuming our time, after all. Isn't that why we're here in the first place?

Have Something to Grow

There are plenty of ways to grow and leverage a business, but we first need to get to the point where we have something to grow. This book is about putting down those foundations and proving the case for your business - with paying clients and reputation that goes before you.

We didn't become an expert within our industry to end up becoming experts at marketing; something I did, and sadly see it happen a lot.

We might want to implement everything we have learned to do, but we also need to be prepared for how long it might take. If we don't have paying clients right now, yes, we can put more time into development but, truthfully, our time is better-spent networking, meeting prospects, talking to them, and becoming experts in our clients' problems; as it is only when we do this that we have the opportunity to pitch our services, gain feedback on our packages and thus win business.

> ## "We didn't become an expert within our industry to end up becoming experts at marketing."

Truthfully, a sale can happen anywhere, simply by chance. It can come via word of mouth recommendation, a new LinkedIn connection, an old colleague, or at the supermarket. A new client will only show up if we are in constant conversation about what you do with our audience.

A sale can take 30-minutes to win, or it can take nine months. As long as you are winning sales appointments, you're in the right place for winning sales. If you're not, something is amiss.

When reviewing the diagram of how people buy, the goal isn't to get stuck trying to complete each section one piece at a time; the goal is to spin around it as fast as you can achieving sales appointments.

Sales Appointments. Sales. Clients. Results.

This is all that matters.

Once you've identified the lead generation strategy that is right for your audience, personality and lifestyle – stick with it and get mastery. Hire a coach to help you secure predictable results you can rely on. But remember, before you hire them, you must take care of everything we've spoken about so far in this book.

As you meet your sales targets and begin generating income, you'll be able to portion off time to develop additional content to help your prospects in their buying journey, knowing that the business is paying you for your time to create it and that you now have enough understanding of your prospects to create something they will really benefit from.

"As you create these assets, your influence will grow, and more prospects will come to you pre-sold, making it easier for you to win each new client and build the business."

As you create these assets, your influence will grow, and more prospects will come to you pre-sold, making it easier for you to win each new client and build the business.

At some points within your business, you may have to opt to work with fewer clients and earn less for a while to give yourself a chance to transform the business. In my second year of business, this is what I had to do. Writing LinkedIn profiles as a core business wasn't sustainable, and I hadn't gone past the point within the business where I could continue as I was.

Instead, I needed to create my training course, my product for prospects that would allow me to stop selling my time and instead sell a product. To achieve this, I had to drop my income target and re-invest the time I would have been writing LinkedIn profiles into developing my course. It was a choice I had to make if I was to grow my business and get out from under the pressure to write LinkedIn Profiles.

There will always be good and bad times

Running your business, there will always be good and bad times, and it is important to understand the season you are in and understand why you have made the choices you have. When I made the adjustments within my business last year to develop my product and took the pay cut, I felt like a failure even though I had made conscious decision to re-direct my time and it was a smart choice.

The important thing is to stay the course.

I've met many business owners who have started their new enterprise with money in the bank, perhaps from redundancy, retirement, savings or even funding. In my experience, this is often more of a negative than a positive as it gives a false sense of security.

"Having money is often more of a negative than a positive when starting a business, as it gives a false sense of security."

Business is about winning sales and delivering results, something that most experts within their industry are not yet skilled in. Even if they are, selling ourselves and our ability to deliver can be a big shift and something most people don't account for. It also takes time to develop a list of prospects and gain enough opportunities to pitch our business and actually win sales. Therefore, there is no time like the present to get on with it.

I have known people to start their businesses and spend months working alone, developing their products and services but never win a sale. They believe that they can't sell their product until they've finished it, and that when they are ready to sell, people will buy. That, then, they'll reap a return on investment for their time. This couldn't be further from the truth.

The truth is that, even though we set sales targets, we won't always meet them. Sometimes, we won't have enough prospects to sell to; sometimes, we will have sales appointments booked but to the wrong type of prospect, meaning no one is buying from us. And, sometimes, we get sick, depressed, or distracted. You can fill in the blanks.

It is at these moments you'll be glad you had the cash set aside to supplement your income and keep you in business. However, relying on your savings as a source of income is not going to work. It only gives you an excuse to delay the inevitable; that you have to get selling your product.

"Learning to hit your sales targets consistently each and every month is a skill that takes time to develop, and you'll want to give yourself the time to do it."

Learning to hit your sales targets consistently each and every month is a skill that takes time to develop, and you'll want to give yourself the time to do it. The last thing you'll want is to miss your sales target and start going into debt as, to regain balance, you'll need to earn it back. To do this, not only will you have to master the skill that failed you and put you in debt, but you will also have to increase your sales target to be able to increase your income and pay the debt back. An additional pressure that will only pull at you, during what can only be described as an ongoing upward learning curve.

Conclusion

At the opening of this book, I began by saying that we have to 'start with the end in mind'. Ultimately, the end you have in mind will be to build a thriving business that fulfils you and, if you're truly an expert in your field, this will mean helping your clients to achieve the very best outcome for them.

The more you focus on delivering value for your clients, the easier this will become. Hopefully, with everything you have learned in this book, you will see how to leverage the time you spend with your clients delivering value, to make things easier for you to continue to win new clients.

Being an expert is not about ego, about building a following, or even about making money. It is about doing what fulfils you most in service of others. The money is just a necessity and a great reward.

If what is written here within these pages resonates with you and you would like further help and support moving your business forward, then I invite to reach out. If you want to accelerate your results and avoid the pitfalls, my advice is to get a coach. One that has walked this path themselves, knows how to evaluate decisions and opportunities and will give you the feedback you need to succeed.

If you feel I could be your coach, please book a LinkedIn Profile & Strategy Review with me at https://theprofile.company/apply-profile-review/

I look forward to working with you.

Final Thoughts

- If you are out meeting your target audience and talking about what you do, you're doing the right thing.

- You don't need to have a perfect website, brand, or brochures to get started talking to your audience.

- As you become an expert in your clients' problems, everything else will fall into place.

- Always package your services into products that are easy to understand starting with low cost to high cost.

- Nothing happens without getting in front of your prospective clients and becoming an expert in their problems.

- You will always be in a process of discovery and change; as long as you keep your eye on the destination, everything else will fall into place.

- The only thing that matters is sales appointments as it is only with them you'll have the opportunity to make a sale!

- LinkedIn is the perfect place to get known and win new clients.

- If you focus on building value for your clients and helping them solve problems, you'll always be on the winning path.

About the Author

Naomi-Rose Everly (previously known as Johnson) is a LinkedIn Expert who began her entrepreneurial career as a Life coach in 2006. After making all classic business mistakes and writing her book Grassroots to Green Shoots about the lessons she learned, Naomi began working for Marketing Help for Coaches.

Determined to rectify her wrongs and master the art of winning new business as a solo-entrepreneur and expert, Naomi was an original delegate of Daniel Priestley's Key Person of Influence course. Shortly after, Naomi became the director of Marketing Help for Coaches in 2011.

It wasn't long before Naomi spotted the advantages LinkedIn afforded and what it could offer. Beginning to find her feet on the topic, Naomi was headhunted to join the world's leading LinkedIn training provider working in partnership with LinkedIn. Naomi ran the Rock Your Profile stand at LinkedIn's Talent Connect conference two years running, before launching TheProfile.Company.

After spending two years reviewing people's LinkedIn profiles while in conversation with the profile owner and writing her second book, "What to Put on Your LinkedIn Profile", Naomi realised that, while people loved her advice, they weren't implementing it because they didn't have time, weren't wordsmiths and were too close to their own business.

Following the principles she now teaches her clients, she started a new business writing LinkedIn profiles for people, which sold out within four months and attracted her big-name clients such as Oracle and individuals from Coke-Cola and Facebook.

However, as Naomi began writing more and more profiles for solo-entrepreneurs who were experts within their industry, Naomi noticed that not only do people tend to undersell themselves on their profile, but their LinkedIn Profile and sales strategy are not set up in a way that will win them business. In fact, most people are missing vital business components that, if put in place, will dramatically change their results.

To help clients resolve this, Naomi wrote an online training course and introduced her one-to-one coaching programme, branding her approach "The Expert Economy" and launching her book by the same name.

In 2024, following a major business and personal rebrand, the book was relaunched as "Magnetise Your Expertise on LinkedIn: How to Become the Only Person Your Clients Want to Work With". Naomi resides on the south coast of England with her two cats Layla and Loki, and works with clients across the globe via Zoom.

Ways to connect with the Author:

If you would like to connect with Naomi-Rose Everly and learn more insights and tips, you can find Podcast episodes on Spotify, Apple, and Google Play by searching for The Expert Economy.

You can also connect with her on LinkedIn www.uk.linkedin.com /in/naomijohnsonuk

Or by emailing naomi@theprofile.company

BECOME THE 'GO-TO' EXPERT IN YOUR INDUSTRY & BUILD A THRIVING BUSINESS

A step-by-step methodology for self-employed business owners to quickly establish their business and get paid their worth.

In our fast-paced, busy lives, we really don't have time to waste when it comes to winning new clients and building our business. What we need is for our name to come up in all the right conversations and our most ideal clients to come to us pre-sold and ready to buy.

Something that, with the right marketing approach, is actually easy to achieve. All you need is a compelling Call-to-Action, clear packages and pricing, and a structured sales conversation.

In this 8-week course, we'll delve deep into your business to uncover the jewels that will help systemise your actions and have clients flowing into your business.

The course is designed to teach you how to get leads and what to do with them.

You will discover exactly how to structure a sales conversation so you can confidently ask the buying question, how to build value in your network so people want to jump on a call with you, how to position yourself as THE industry expert, and pitch your business in a way that makes you easy to refer business too.

THE END OF THE COURSE, YOU'LL HAVE:

• A step-by-step methodology that allows you to quickly win new clients.

• A roadmap that shows you exactly where you are in building your journey, so you know what to focus on.

• A compelling Call-to-Action that has your prospects eager to speak to you.

• A sales script that allows you to stay in control of the conversation, explore your prospects' issues, and decide together if working together is the right solution.

• Your non-ideal prospects and those that don't sign up to your programme eager to your ideal prospects about you.

• Clarity on exactly where to focus your attention each day to get results and balance your time.

• A product eco-system that allows your prospects to build a relationship with you in their own time, leaving you free to work with the clients that are ready.

• Packages priced correctly that fit your target markets budget and ensure you get paid your worth.

• A LinkedIn strategy focused on booking a sales appointment with ideal prospects.

• A LinkedIn content strategy that will open up an entirely new pool of prospects who previously weren't looking for your solution.

• A strategy that will position you in the minds of your prospect as THE expert within your industry who they absolutely have to work with.

• A LinkedIn profile that builds rapport with your network, pitches your solution so everyone can understand what you do.

Visit: www.TheProfile.Company or email naomi@theprofile.company

Other Books by the Author

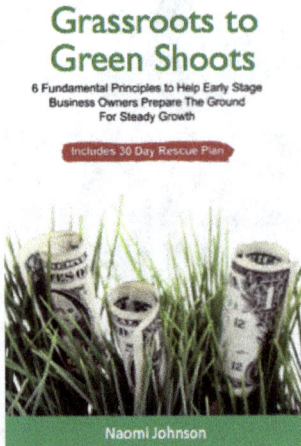

Grassroots to Green Shoots

6 Fundamental Principles to Help Early Stage
Business Owners Prepare The Ground
For Steady Growth

Includes 30 Day Rescue Plan

Naomi Johnson

Grassroots to Green Shoots

ISBN-978-0-9568055-1-5

In 2008, after a catalogue of mistakes, Naomi Johnson had to
walk away from her coaching business, having invested three
hard years of blood, sweat, and tears. At a breaking point, she
was subletting her bedroom, sleeping on the sofa and eating
baked beans for every meal, opening a can with a knife
because she couldn't afford a new tin opener. Her creditors
were phoning seven times a day, and she had no peace.

In this book, Naomi deals head-on with the 'Get Rich Quick'
industry and speaks frankly about what it really takes to be
successful. She reveals the secret to making the transition from
work to full-time entrepreneurship, how to find extra money in
your monthly budget to invest in your business, and how to
work out whether your business model can really meet your
financial targets and get you the life you want.

Based around the wisdom she learned from her own mistakes, Naomi holds nothing back as she shares first-hand from her own journey. By reading this book, you will avoid many of the unspoken pitfalls successful business gurus don't think to tell you – things that, if left unchecked, will mean it's 'Game Over' before you know it.

This book is perfect for the small business entrepreneurs who are starting to realise that the entrepreneur revolution may not be quite as easy as the ride it's been billed as. If you are starting a new business, this book is a must-read.

5* Refreshingly Honest

I found Naomi's book a refreshing change from the larger than life writing we are so often fed from business writers, which is often so hard for regular business owners to identify with. Naomi writes in a down to earth way for real people who are dealing with real-life business issues that are starved of practical ways to move from a to b. She shares much of her own tough journey which I believe will resonate with many struggling to survive when times get hard and gives hope that with the right set of tools and decisions things can be turned around. I found myself nodding as I read it.
-   Verified Amazon Customer

5* Invaluable Insights and Advice

This is a very useful book with some great tools, advice and calls to action. Naomi is frank and honest and in her 30-day action plan focuses on removing the foot off the accelerator to stop you digging a deeper hole and resurface with some sanity. She also gets you to think about some very simple yet paradigm-shifting ideas if you want to pursue coaching as a career. Thank you, Naomi, for telling your story, highlighting the pitfalls and explaining why and how even great ones fall, and what to do about it.
-   Verified Amazon Customer

What to Put on Your LinkedIn Profile

ISBN-978-0-95-68055-3-9

Your LinkedIn profile is your window to the world. In an era of information overload, our human brains are programmed to stereotype and pigeonhole people in a matter of seconds, so if you want to make a lasting impression, having an engaging LinkedIn profile that speaks directly to the audience is imperative.

Having conducted hundreds of profile review, author Naomi Johnson knows that most LinkedIn profiles do not reflect the brilliance of the individuals behind them. In this book, Naomi delves into what separates an 'OK' profile from an outstanding one.

The Ultimate Guide to Writing Your LinkedIn Profile

Everything you need to write your own LinkedIn Profile, so prospects come to you pre-sold and ready to buy!

In an era of information overload, our human brains are programmed to **stereotype and pigeonhole people** in a **matter of seconds,** so if we want to make a **lasting impression**, having an engaging LinkedIn profile that **speaks directly to our audience is imperative.**

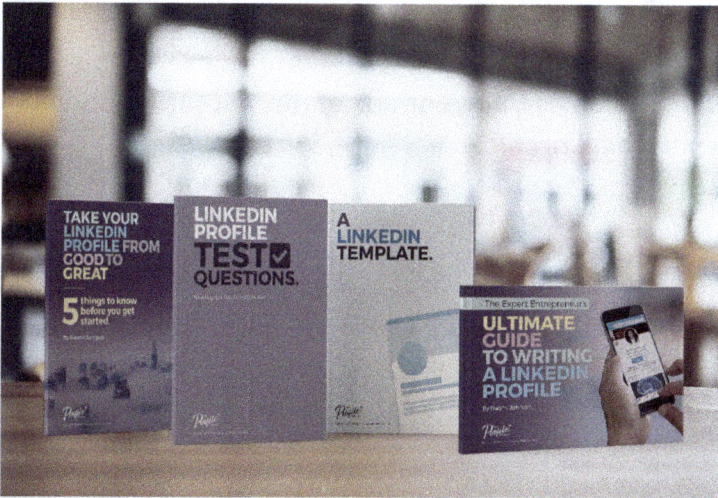

In this kit, you will learn:

How to approach your LinkedIn Profile as an Entrepreneur compared to a job seeker.

How to write your LinkedIn Profile so you stand out in your industry and prospect come to your sales appointments eager speak you.

Questions to consider about your business and marketing direction before you even think to start writing.

How to use each section of your LinkedIn Profile to the maximum.

A step-by-step guide to writing your LinkedIn Profile, so you don't waste time.

Receive key pointers for writing your profile that will really kick-start the process.

Guidance on asking your target market for feedback on your new profile.

Plus, you'll be able to rate your own LinkedIn Profile Assessment Quiz.

Includes: 28-page Guide, LinkedIn Profile Template, Profile Quiz, Report: 'Taking Your Profile from Good to Great'.

Visit:
www.theprofile.company/ultimate-linkedin-profile-guide

www.ingramcontent.com/pod-product-compliance
Lightning Source LLC
Chambersburg PA
CBHW061235220326
41599CB00028B/5429